Talking to the Dead in Suburbia

Brigitta—

4/09

An Ordinary Woman with an Extraordinary Gift

God Bless—

Anna L. Raimondi

Anna L. Raimondi

INFINITY
PUBLISHING.COM

*Copy-editing provided by Denise Sabol.
Cover design by Willa Ratner.*

ISBN 0-7414-5182-4

Published by:

INFINITY
PUBLISHING.COM

*1094 New DeHaven Street, Suite 100
West Conshohocken, PA 19428-2713
Info@buybooksontheweb.com
www.buybooksontheweb.com
Toll-free (877) BUY BOOK
Local Phone (610) 941-9999
Fax (610) 941-9959*

Printed in the United States of America

Printed on Recycled Paper

Published February 2009

Dedication

To my husband, who has watched my gifts grow and my life change. Your love and support and patience (!) gave me the confidence and courage to follow my path and write this book. I love you.

Table of Contents

Prologue 1

Introduction - And in the Beginning, There was ME, a
Little Pencil on the Paper of Life. 9

Part I: - Talking to the Dead 13

Welcome to My World 15

A Mere Woman in Suburbia 28

Living with a Medium – What a Trip! 37

Walking with the Angels 47

There are No Coincidences 59

Who is this Person Interrupting my Prayers? 68

Hey, are you Listening? 72

Here I am, in the Zone 77

Coffee, Muffins and the Dead! 83

So You Want? But What Do You Need? 90

Who Were You? 99

I Just Keep Getting in the Way! 105

Love is the Beginning and the End – It is the All 109

I Want to Speak with My Mother! 114

No Crystal Ball Here 120

We are All Children of the Universe, Both the
Greatest of Teachers and Students. 131

Part II: - Making the Connection...................................... 141

So You Want to Talk to the Spirit World....................... 143

Walking Through Life with Eyes Wide Open................ 146

Meditation - The Transition from Head to Heart 149

Can You Hear Me? I Am Listening. 156

Until We Meet Again 163

Works Cited.. 165

Acknowledgements 166

Prologue

Writing in the "In-Between" Times

This book, written during the "in-between" times, came together amid attending little league baseball games, school field trips, car rides to the doctor and the vet, playing taxi cab driver for my sons as I brought them to and from school, making breakfast, lunch and dinner, cleaning the house, grocery shopping, helping with school projects, spending time with husband – what little time was left for us – making a website, organizing a retreat, starting a business, helping my son prepare to go off to college and those precious moments spent crying and laughing at the pain and the happiness of watching my children walk into their futures. And, that is only the half of it; my life is much more complicated. Yet, like you, I am not a superhero, but rather, a mere mortal, a mother and wife, raising a family in suburbia and living my life the best that I can.

A few years ago the corporate world began using the buzzword "multi-task." Commercials hit the airwaves depicting executives with telephones glued to their ears, while typing on their laptops and listening to colleagues simultaneously. Although, this visual portrayal of our American work ethic is admirable (bordering on lunacy!), anyone with a family knows full well that "multi-tasking" is not a new phenomenon. Most of us do not have maids, cooks and drivers to take care of our family while we are out playing tennis all day. We all have performed multi-tasking as we carry down the dirty clothes to the washing machine and turn around to carry the washed clothes up and put them away, as we balance the phone on our ears so that we can hear the guidance counselor at the high school while pulling on our shirts all in ten minutes and way before 9:00 a.m.! And that is not all. We continue this practice, as we load our children into our cars, drive them to school, while we drink coffee, eat breakfast, comb our hair, listen to our child's book report and give our well thought out feedback! And, there is more. Many of us, after dropping off the children at school, race off to the office for seven hours or so of work! Sound familiar? Of course it does. It is how we live. In our society multi-tasking is the rule of thumb.

Truth be told, as I am putting my words on these pages, dinner is cooking in the oven, my younger son is upstairs calling down to me, with something very important (but not important enough to actually come down the stairs!) while my other son is calling on the phone to ask me to pick him up from his wrestling practice. So, I must stop typing, break my train of thought and take care of my children as I remember to breathe. Being a mom is a balancing act, or more accurately a circus act. "See Anna on the high wire, carrying the groceries, speaking on the cell phone held between her shoulder and her ear while a child hangs onto her leg for dear life. Will she fall before reaching the end? A little bit more, and she will be there. Hooray, she made it to the other side!" For many of us, this is life. I, for one, would not want it any other way. It is my life. I love my children, my husband, my dogs, and my life. Yet, there is more to my life than meets the eye; much more than a simple balancing act.

Given all the blissful chaos in my life, in order to get the entirety of my thoughts committed to paper, some of the minor and more mundane aspects of my daily existence had to be put on the back burner. I am sure all the employees at the TJ Maxx store in Norwalk, Connecticut are surely missing me these days! The hour or so a day I usually spent shopping and wasting time while waiting for my sons' guitar lessons or baseball practices to end, has been replaced with putting my views on paper. My husband is thrilled at the prospect of saving the money usually wasted on unnecessary shopping. Yet, in the broader scheme of things, putting my thoughts into words, describing my journey and sharing who I am on paper, has been saving more than money. My sanity has been salvaged and a more profound realization of who I truly am has emerged. Sharing the core of my existence; explaining my God-given gifts and re-walking my path, has afforded me a clearer view of my life's purpose. This experience has broadened my perspective on my own life and propelled me to write from my soul.

In doing so, I hope my uniqueness as a creature of this planet shines through. Our libraries and bookstores are overflowing with books that concentrate on the spirit world. However, these numerous tomes and articles span a vast array and assortment of spiritual topics; diverse and special. Each author, each storyteller, dedicates and imparts a piece of his or her heart and soul to their work.

Yet, storytellers are not all lofty and distinguished people. Some are; some are not. For that matter, we are all storytellers, with our own personal tale to divulge. And, collectively, many of us hope and pray that our story will touch someone deeply and move him or her to introspection and a place of healing. This is my prayer for the words that fill these pages. I am prompted to write this book not only to share my story to help spread the word about the gifts of the Spirit, but also to help pry open your eyes to your own gifts and to give you the courage to step out and put your gifts to good use.

Scattered among the forthcoming chapters is my quest to share my gifts through stories from my life and techniques that I utilize to listen and talk to those among the spirit world. There is no one right way or wrong way to heal or communicate with those on the other side. My way of funneling healing from the Divine and conversing with the spirit world may provide you with some tools for your spiritual toolbox and support you on your own path. You may use these tools and methods; or design a whole new set of protocols that work for you. These tools may just be food for thought for you, a beginning point. We are all unique; whatever works for you is what you should do. Just remember, please, if you do enter this work to carry integrity and sincerity on your sleeve and in your heart. Speak the words that you hear at your deepest core; and separate yourself, your ego, from the equation. Discernment is necessary since we are not compelled to relate everything heard, seen or felt. More importantly, never ever fake or falsify information just to make someone feel good or in some way elevate your ego. If you live by this rule, your gifts will blossom into blessed flowers that fill the fields of your life with beauty and virtue only attained by connection with the Truth of heaven.

As I lay myself before you, my hope is that my life's work can teach, heal and expand a tiny segment of the world. Although writing about oneself is always therapeutic, the mission of this book is to assist the universe by reaching out and teaching through the example of my life's journey. Mine is a normal existence with extraordinary experiences that may in some way heal and help others; maybe you. As a "hands on" healer, I recognize this writing as just another "hands on" modality. As my fingertips tap away on the keyboard and my energy flows onto the pages, from me directly to you, there is a reciprocal healing going on. I invite you to draw this energy into your being and allow your mind and soul to expand with each word, paragraph and chapter set before you. Of course, the responsibility lies within you; it is all up to you. This type of healing is innocuous and does not involve scalpels or intrusive examinations. There may be pain, if you delve to the center of your being, yet the grand finale may result in your energy body and soul being filled with love, peace and a bit more understanding of your own existence.

It is helpful if you stay "mindful" and present as you read along. Think about how the words I convey affect you during your daily life. Be mindful of the synchronicities that occur each and every day of your life. It is important to be aware of these twists of fate as much as possible. For instance, do you recognize and are you cognizant of the distinct reason that you feel compelled to read this book? The reason may be obvious or it may be elusive to you at this very moment. As your fingers continue to turn one page onto another, the motivation for you to persevere through my journey may become crystal clear. Your purpose may be to open up to your own gifts, to understand the life of a medium in today's society or you may be encouraged by some other inspiration of which only you are familiar. Whatever the reason may be, by virtue of picking up this book and allowing the energy of my words to fill your senses, we are merged energetically.

If you carefully read this book, you may notice that certain techniques, feelings and suggestions are repeated. Also, a piece of a story may be told and picked up later in the book. Forgive my nagging (I am Italian and can be bossy!), but the repetitions are necessary to convey the full gist of communication with the other side. If you are saying to yourself as you read the excerpt, "She said this already, I got it, I get it!" Then all is good; I accomplished my goal.

It is true that in the sharing of my life with you, we share a common energy cord. You may feel the energy of my love, my life and the essence of my soul as it touches each page. As your eyes absorb the words on the pages set before you, my energy and your energy will mesh. Thus, a bond, a thread of connectivity, will form between our hearts. In that uniting, something wonderful and miraculous may transpire. Yes, maybe even a miracle. A miracle does not have to be an earth-shattering event. It is said of Jesus, and stands true of Buddha and the other enlightened Masters who have walked this earth, 'the greatest miracle that ever was and still remains, is altering the Heart of humankind.' This is the miracle, which melts fear and the walls that we erect between each other and replaces them with compassion and understanding. Therefore, any miracle that you may experience does not have to be spectacular; but will certainly be enlightening. It may open your eyes, ears, heart and soul to a world that you have yet to enter; or perhaps you have not entered as fully as is necessary for your soul. It may give you the confidence and ability to rise to your birth right as the bearer of miracles.

Ezra Pound once said that a "book should be a ball of light in one's hand." As you read this book, hold it not only as a ball of light and my energy, but accept the Divine light that shines onto the pages. I surrender myself as a vehicle through which this Power flows. Without this Power, the words on these pages are just ink marks. The Power translates the ink marks into words of inspiration. Also, my undying faith in this Power releases the underlying vivacity of my spirit, my soul and the Spirit of the entire universe. As you read this book, or for that matter any book, be conscious of your own energy shifting and give yourself permission to absorb the great Divine Power of the universe. Allow yourself to transform, transmute and grow with this energy.

Do not be surprised, as you read this book, if you notice the physical manifestations of the energy that is flowing through you. Blisters may appear, or you may experience frequent urination or an increase in sweating; the aroma of sweet fragrances may surround you as a sense of psychic knowing becomes apparent; you may have feelings of butterflies fluttering in the pit of your stomach or tingling at the base of your skull. It may also manifest as a preoccupa-tion with the subject matter and a desire to learn and read more. This is a pure and undisputable link to the universal energy and to my spirit. These physical manifestations are wonderful in that they validate our unity at a level that involves our minds as well as our hearts.

These energy manifestations can happen to all of us. As a matter of fact, it has happened to me. A few years ago, I was in the middle of reading a book about the life of a particular energy healer. After retiring the book to my nightstand, my family and I embarked upon a trip to the Dominican Republic. While in the Dominican Republic, I noticed that there were blisters erupting like mini volcanoes on the palm of my left hand. I thought that the appearance of these blisters was rather peculiar. So, after much thought, and not reaching a conclusive answer as to the reason for these blisters, I put my hand under my husband's nose to show him and ask his opinion.

My husband in his engaging, yet sarcastic way, said, "Well it certainly is not from manual labor, or housework!" He is not always funny but he speaks the truth.

"It is probably because I hold the leash too tightly when I walk the dogs." I countered without really thinking.

"When do you walk the dogs? You open the back door and let them run outside!"

Of course he was right. I was just searching for an answer. In reality, I had not walked the dogs in about two years.

Although I did not know the reason behind the appearance of the blisters, I was consciously and acutely aware of them worsening and then, as though they were contagious, they began to appear on my right hand. These skin eruptions did not cause me any pain, just a little tightening, so my fascination was simply an attempt to understand and find the cause. No clues were provided and so, finally, the search was dismissed and my attention was refocused on getting a tan and enjoying the time with my family.

And so it was, weeks later, as bursts of red, yellow and blue sparks shot from the fireplace in our family room, enveloping the room in a warm and protective glow, I sat down in my most comfortable chair to relax with the book that I had left behind when we embarked on our vacation. A couple of pages into the chapter, the author described how some people, while reading that book, experienced blisters and other physical manifestations, as his energy joined with their energy field. This was nothing short of astounding and was validation that his energy was reaching me over the distance between us and acting to manifest as blisters on my hands. I recognized that the words that I was reading were sinking in at a much deeper level than just mental stimulation. Since that time, whenever and whatever I read; conduct healing sessions; connect with the spirit world; or even as I write this, I feel a growing tightness spreading across my palms. Frequently, my palms will blister just as they did in the Dominican Republic. This is a straightforward, undeniable sign to me that I am on the right path; that I am universally and spiritually connecting with others. I really love validation. That's just me.

And so, let my journey unravel before you as we make our connection through this great and wondrous universe.

Introduction

And in the Beginning, There was ME, a Little Pencil on the Paper of Life.

I am a little pencil in the hand of a writing God who is sending a love letter to the world.
Mother Teresa

She parked her car in the church parking lot, opened the car door and swung her stocking clad legs onto the cement pavement. The clickety-click of her high heels reverberated through the quiet night as she walked toward the school building where the religious education classes were taught. She wore a bright red suit; the skirt hitting just above the knees as was the style in 1990. Her hair was a deep mahogany, not touched by the grey that she would lament and fuss about in the future. Although she was only twenty-nine she felt as tired as a person twice her age. After a long day at work in New York City; she hopped on a train to the station in a town nearby to where she lived; then jumped into her car to make a ten-minute trip to her house. Upon arriving at her house, she quickly parked the car and literally ran into her house, kissed her infant son, said a quick hello to the babysitter, ate an apple and ran back out the door and back into the car. Life was too busy. She felt extremely crunched for time. Her day certainly was not long enough and yet at the same time it was too long. Her husband, with whom she had only five minutes to speak that day, would be home soon. When she returned later that night, the baby and her husband would be nestled on the sofa together, fast asleep.

Pushing open one of the double glass doors, she walked into the school building. She was greeted by her mother, who ran the religious education program for the parish along with her father. The program was for public school children who did not receive religious instruction during the normal school day.

Her mother greeted her with, "You are teaching the eighth grade confirmation class. Your father gave you the tough kids again."

She inwardly groaned. Her father always gave her the tough, troubled teens. Of course, tough is relative. This was not an inner city, but a quiet suburb of New York City. Tough usually meant that the kids had emotional scars due to divorce, death in the family or lack of financial means to keep up in the wealthy upper middle class environment in which they lived. This translated into a lack of respect for authority, sarcasm and, by no stretch of the imagination, a totally unruly group. But her parents assigned her to teach these teenagers because they felt that she could handle it! Terrific!

She quickly walked up the narrow staircase to her classroom and pushed open the heavy wooden door. The kids barely looked up to acknowledge her presence but instead continued to talk, standing here and there in the classroom or sitting on the tops of old, worn out desks. Showing no sign of annoyance, she put her books on the teacher's desk in the front center of the room, and just stared at them and counted. There were fifteen fourteen year old kids milling around in the classroom before her; all there by no choice of their own. She leaned against the desk, crossed her legs at her ankle, until one by one, they lifted or turned their heads and noticed her. She waited patiently and when she felt that they were fully aware of her presence and wondering what was going through her mind, she said in a quiet yet clear voice, "I love you."

At once, the room became abnormally silent. "What?" A dark headed boy in a tee shirt and torn jeans asked while he looked around the room as a sarcastic smirk spread on his face.

"I worked all day, but instead of being at home spending time with my baby and my husband, I am here; so, therefore, I must love you. Each one of you carries Divinity in your hearts and in your souls. I see that in you, and I love you. That is the reason I am here."

She had won their full and undivided attention as they all began to sit at the desks around the room, their eyes not leaving her face. As she walked through the aisles she glanced at each one of them taking in the essence of their energy as it swirled around her. When she spoke again it was with strength and conviction.

"This year each one of you will choose to become a Roman Catholic; a soldier of the church. It is a decision you make spiritually, intellectually and emotionally. There are no coincidences; you are in this class for a reason. This class might be a little unconventional in that I invite you to listen to what I have to say, and pick and choose what makes sense to you or what feels right. It is okay to question and doubt; I invite you to ask questions."

One boy, who sat by himself in the back of the room, his legs crossed defiantly on the desk in front of him, spoke out brashly, the anger and pain mingling with his words.

"This is a bunch of bull. Divinity is in all of us! Yeah, right. Lady, don't be so high and mighty, you don't live in my house! Where is God in my alcoholic father when he decides to terrorize my mother and me?"

And with these harsh words that bespoke a cruel world, the class began and these disorderly teenagers became the seekers of the light and the Truth.

That young woman is me almost twenty years ago. Now, as I sit here and write, I realize that once again I am sacrificing a piece of my life. I am volunteering a piece of who I am to you; as my family, which has grown to two sons and two dogs, run and play ball outside on a warm Autumn day in New England. Yet, I sit with my laptop warming my legs in the comfort of my family room and pour out my heart and soul because I love you. Like I said so many years ago to those young teenagers, take what you will from the words that flow from me; take what make sense to you. Do not be afraid to question and look beyond the words on the page and realize that it was all written with love for you. Maybe, just maybe, if you aren't a seeker of the light and the Truth already, like those kids so many years ago, you will be moved to seek them out now.

Part I:

Talking to the Dead

You see, death is not the grave as many people think.
It is another phenomenized form of life.
Edgar Cayce

Welcome to My World

A life is not important except in the impact it has on other lives.
Jackie Robinson

Every book has a voice. In writing this book, my voice rings loud and clear. Therefore, it is important to know my background, to get acquainted with me, the person, not just the healer or spiritual medium. In doing so, the ultimate comprehension of my journey will be more apparent. You might notice as you flip through these pages, that although I am an ordinary person, I have had tremendous experience in the realm of the "not so ordinary." And, underlying it all, I maintain a strong faith in a Power that is among, within, and yet, beyond us. It is this Power, this God, and a universe of angels, elders, ascended masters, prophets and saints who work in conjunction with me to heal and help others. I certainly am not great enough to do this work alone; yet the God that moves through me is absolute in His/Her greatness. As I share myself with you, my spiritual truth will become obvious.

To me, God, the mother/father Divine is the Alpha and the Omega of every moment, set apart as a Power of magnificent intensity and magnitude. That is the foundation of my belief system in a nutshell. It is not necessary to have the same beliefs that I have; but as you get to know me, you might like to know on what basis I speak my truth. Further, I believe with all my heart that God is with me and in me and moves through me. Thus, when healings occurs via my physical and spiritual being, through my words or through my work as a "hands on healer" or as a "spiritual medium", it is God's healing love that conducts the healings and not me. It is God that opens up the channels for me to see clairvoyantly. I am a willing vehicle of the Divine Power, working in direct partnership. I believe that we all carry the DNA of God within our souls and it encompasses all that is good within all of us. It is all that is virtuous within our world. We are all vehicles of healing; we just go about it in different ways. We all possess a unique gift. As the saying goes, "Different strokes for different folks." Yet, this Divine DNA along with our own unique gift of healing connects us to each other.

I have come to recognize and even profess that I am a "healer." It has taken many years for me to be able to express those words and give myself such a lofty label. It is not often that you meet someone who actually blurts out "I am a healer and what do you do?" or "Nice to meet you, need some healing?" However, "healer" is a misnomer, but for lack of a better word, it is used to describe the healing Power moving through mere humans. In our culture if one declares their profession to be a medical doctor or therapist, one is admitting to have many years of education and intense medical acumen and expertise under his or her belt. These professionals are correctly viewed as bonafide professional "healers." Yet, in contrast, my education in the field of "energy healing" or "spiritual healing" has been a life experience. Much of what I do cannot be academically pursued. It is an ability that resides deep within my soul that has been screaming to be released my whole life. As I grow and accept who and what I am, this gift flourishes and matures, transmutes and grows toward what it was always meant to be; like a flower reaching for the warm rays of the sun. The acceptance of our unique gifts, and the permission to let them flourish, is exciting and, much of the time, life altering. Sooner or later, many of us recognize the need to "just go for it" and be who we were meant to be; whether or not our society sanctions our uniqueness and who and what we are. I hope reading this book instills a fire of courage deep within your soul and motivates you to allow your personal gifts to grow so that you can be all that you are meant to be.

So, exactly, what is it that I profess to be? Well, at the risk of being repetitious and vague, I declare nothing except that I am truly a conduit through which universal energy, love and Divine intervention, knowledge and compassion flows. We are all pieces of a giant jigsaw puzzle that interrelates and helps the other pieces fit. We do not act alone; we need the other pieces, we need the universe, the ultimate end-all to make this work. Therefore, we are nothing without the Puzzle Maker. This holds true with energy and spiritual work. To believe that my energy is the tool and the ointment that heals would be to make myself into the ultimate all. I am not Divinity personified. I, like everyone else, carry Divinity within my soul. Yet, I have accepted my fate and allow this Divinity to work in me and through me in various ways.

In my case, I did not wake up one day and say, "wow I am a healer." Rather, it was a lifetime stride toward the eventual realization that I was born to do the work of a healer. Waking up and actually opening my eyes to the platter of spiritual fruit laid before me was cathartic. It was always there and with me my whole life, ripening right under my nose. In accepting my truth, I permitted myself to taste the sweet juices that ran from the plate. I was seeing and tasting for the first time who I was born to be; of the life path that I was destined to walk. It is amazing how most of us go through life with such wonderful and extraordinary experiences happening all the time and yet do not really see what is going on; our eyes are covered with blinders made of fear. We see but we do not see. We understand but we do not understand. We all need to finally open our eyes and keep them open to fully view life one moment at a time and to live in the moment. It is important to experience each moment and to see beyond what our eyes are showing us. One day, this awakening happened to me.

In the movie "Contact", Jodi Foster's character, Ellie, an astronomer, delivers a monologue before Congress which describes her belief in something greater than us. These simple yet powerful words echo in the chambers of my heart as I share them with you. In the scene, she is asked why she won't concede her position about another life form in the universe. She passionately answers:

> Because I can't. I had an experience I cannot prove, I cannot even explain it, but everything that I know as a human being, everything that I am, tells me that it was real. I was part of something wonderful, something that changed me forever; a vision of the Universe that tells us undeniably how tiny, and insignificant, and how rare and precious we all are. A vision that tells us we belong to something that is greater than ourselves. That we are not, that none of us are, alone. I wish I could share that. I wish that everyone, if even for one moment, could feel that awe, and humility, and the hope. But... that continues to be my wish.

Wow, isn't that terrific? This reflection mirrors what I feel in my heart as I write these words. Many of us have had encounters that defy our intellect and yet, we know they are authentic. The overwhelming ardor of the moment resonates and sings in our souls. The tremendous love is so great that it is all consuming. And we know we are not alone. And in that realization, and that moment, we are defined and often changed. I, like Ellie, would like to share the awe, humility and hope that I have taken away from these experiences and I hope you, in turn, can learn how to open your heart and soul to do the work that you were meant to do on this planet.

As Ellie describes, we are small and insignificant in light of the universe, yet we are special. And it is in that moment of awareness that we know beyond a shadow of a doubt, beyond all reasoning and intellectual understanding that we are so special and that we are never left alone. Also, in that moment, we recognize and accept the gifts that have been given to us. Yet, it is the initiation of courage that is essential in order to fully realize and develop our gifts of the Spirit and to share our uniqueness with the world.

Courage is a big word. It means stepping out, without fear of condemnation or ridicule. It is a bit nerve-wracking. Imagine this, you walk into a cocktail party with your spouse and see a man across the room conversing with a group of people. You turn to your spouse and say, "That guy over there is very insecure. His mother really did a job on him. He is having a difficult time having that conversation with those people. Poor guy. Should I tell him that there is an older man standing next to him prompting him to stand his ground?" Yes, that would be an act of courage, or insanity. Well, as you can well imagine, when I related those words to my husband, Vinny, recently at a party being hosted by a co-worker of his, the look of pure horror on his face was nothing short of comical. Vinny's stunned, and yes frightened, reaction was as though Freddie Krueger had walked into the room! By no means did he want me to say anything to this stranger. Courage is one thing; I guess appropriateness is another. And, embarrassing the family is a definite no-no. So, I learned to use my "gift of sight", for lack of a better term, wisely and "appropriately." Of course, albeit Vinny's reaction, if I had gone over to that man and blurted out all I saw, he might have been intrigued but he may have thought that I was Looney Tunes. I still have to operate within societal rules and sometimes keep my courage in check.

You may be wondering how this gift manifested itself for me. And so I am compelled to tell my story. Some believe that we begin life with a blueprint written and accepted by our higher selves or our souls. Although we have free will, the blueprint loosely establishes lessons that we must learn to raise ourselves to the level that is necessary to attain heaven, or nirvana. Although, as Robert Frost so eloquently spoke of in "A Road Less Traveled", we ultimately choose our paths along a guideline or road map that is individualized for each one of us. Each of us chooses our own road; sometimes the road less traveled. Following this premise, in adhering to our blueprint, our souls also choose the family into which we are born. If that is the case, then it stands to reason that we also select the time and the era that our souls are to emerge onto this planet.

That being said, my spirit entered this world on a snowy morning at the beginning of the 1960's in a small hospital in Brooklyn, New York. This was a time of tremendous turmoil and change in the United States, as well as the world. As I emerged from my mother's womb, the world was in a state of pure chaos but with the underlying hope of change and progress. The world was entering the dimension of the unknown on many different fronts. Communism was raging abroad, while humanitarianism and racial acceptance were spreading across the United States. Fidel Castro and Nikita Khruschev were controlling the masses in Cuba and the Soviet Union, while great men like Martin Luther King, Jr. spoke of peace and racial equality. And, the United States had a new young President who trumpeted the hope of a better tomorrow, as many young Americans were exhaling the last breath of their lives on a battlefield thousands of miles from the land and the country in which they were born.

While war raged in Vietnam, killing thousands, people protested in the States while others clung to JFK's famous words "Ask not what your country can do for you, but what you can do for your country." The division in the United States had reached a level that had not been seen since the Civil War. So while some burned the flag, others took them up and waved them high. However, amidst all this confusion and pain, people still clung to the hope of a better day. And with this mindset, the quest for the unknown was explored. A program to explore space and other planets enthralled the country and led us to new ways of thinking. And great minds gave birth to promising technology that ultimately led to the age of computerization. In retrospect, the belief that there was more to life than just what we physically saw with the naked eye was monumental on many levels. These changes were extraordinary and unprecedented.

And so, in the midst of the turmoil, or maybe in spite of it, my very young parents welcomed their first child. And on my birthday, the lyrics that flowed from the radio rang out notes of hope for peace and brotherly love. The melody was of endurance in the face of adversity while the mellifluous harmony softy, yet powerfully echoed healing throughout the country and the world. As with most healing, there is usually pain and conflict before the path to happiness and health can be reached. The same premise held true with the social unrest that held captive my country. The road to peace was a difficult one, paved with blood, confusion and discordance, both here and abroad,. The hearts, minds and emotions of the American people were crushed. We were a broken people. But, as Americans have proven their resilience many times in the past, the healing process began. It is of no coincidence that this marked the beginnings of my life.

After the first eighteen months of my life, my parents moved from the city to a suburb of New York. My father, who had passing thoughts of becoming a priest before he met my mother, became active in the local Roman Catholic

Church as a layperson. This was also a time of great change in the church amid the political upheaval over the Vietnam War and unrest in American society. People screamed for change in all the institutions that affected their lives and began to accept the "unknown."

And, the "unknown" began to appear to me. I remember seeing images and feeling the spirit world from the time I was a toddler, even before my leap into the "healing ministry" of the church. At two years old, I announced to my parents that I had an imaginary friend. To this day, I can see this "friend" although to everyone else he was invisible. He was a big, Old English Sheep Dog that followed me everywhere and protected me. Some members of my extended family thought that I was in need of deep psychiatric help! Once, my uncle tried to convince my parents to seek professional help for me. It was a summer-time party and my aunt and uncle had come in from Brooklyn to visit us on Long Island. After chatting a bit with my parents, my Uncle Vito decided to sit down on a lawn chair. As he eased his body onto the chair, I started to yell that he was going to sit on my friend. Uncle Vito was startled and immediately jumped away from the "empty" chair. My parents laughed and told him that my imagination was healthy that my "make believe" friends were a sign of a creative mind and an indication of intelligence. Well, Uncle Vito stayed very far from me. He was not convinced that I was just a creative child and believed that my parents should be contacting an institution for the mentally deranged.

Maybe Uncle Vito was correct; maybe it was not my imagination. Perhaps, just maybe, this friend, this protector of sorts, was the first of many spirits and guides I would encounter throughout my life. Given the clarity of the image of this "friend" in my mind to this day, and the feeling of peace and comfort it conjures, I am convinced that my Old English Sheep Dog friend was one of my many spirit guides. He presented himself as larger than life to me, a small child, and therefore was able to instill a feeling of protection and comfort for me when fear loomed large.

As the days turned into years, I remember seeing angels floating around the ceilings in my family home. I also remember little gifts appearing here and there without any explanation. My parents, being very open to supernatural phenomenon, never told me that I was creating this in my mind, but rather accepted these occurrences as something beyond all of us. They did not put too much emphasis on these events, yet, did not discount or discredit my tales as simply the imagination of a girl. In their acceptance, my gifts were permitted to evolve and expand.

However, my parents, who subscribed to Roman Catholicism, were intent on providing a Catholic religious foundation for me and enrolled me in the nearby Catholic School. I attended parochial school for two years during which the Council of Vatican II loosened some of the rules of the church. To a young child this change was very confusing. Yet, in retrospect it proved to be a great learning experience. It taught me that life is fluid and it changes constantly in all areas of our existence. My parochial school experience also ingrained in me an underlying knowledge that religion is something that is established and governed by people. By witnessing this change, I was afforded the luxury to separate religion from spirituality at a young age. Divinity remained unchanged whether or not nuns wore habits or dresses.

In September 1966, my first year in school, my teacher, Sister Paul, wore the traditional long black habit of the nuns of the Dominican order at that time, with matching black and white veil and heavy rosary beads attached to the waistband of the skirt. By the end of that very same year in school, this outfit was replaced with a knee length grey habit and her name was changed to Angela. Shockingly, she went from Sister Paul, to Sister Angela to Miss Raymond when she ultimately left the order, at the end of the school year, to pursue her journey as a layperson. Try to explain this to a seven year old child who is acutely aware of the world around her! It just did not make sense to me. This resulted in a demystification of the clergy to me. It taught me that nuns and priests were just people pursuing their own dreams, following their own path, special in their vocation but just like the rest of us. Even in my immature, naïve mind, I learned to differentiate the people that represented religion as separate from God. In my naiveté it was clear to me that God was God and everyone else were helpers, just people.

Moreover, the leaders of the church decided that it was no longer necessary to "put on the Sunday attire" and get dressed up for mass anymore. As shocking as it was to some, people began to wear denim jeans to services! The feeling was that God did not care about the outerwear of his children, but more about what they wore in their hearts. We were forced to look inside ourselves, into the place where our love of God and the seat of our spirituality resided. The formality of Catholicism was changing just as often as my mother changed the color of her hair in those days and people were led to the deeper meaning of their belief in the Almighty and what truly mattered. I am not sure that was the intent of the fathers of the church, but the Spirit moves in ways that are sometimes unknown to us as we go through the motions. These changes eventually brought many of us out from under the cloak of established practices and into to a true connection with the Spirit of the God.

Along with the change in the church, more and more high school graduates were choosing to attend college, which, in turn, bred generations of intellectual rebels. No longer were precepts accepted on face value, but dissected piece-by-piece and analyzed. The simple acceptance of life was overthrown by a generation that viewed life as a challenge and an entity to actively pursue and understand on all levels. For the first time, there were masses of people, questioning their belief systems on a deeper level than their parents. We did not accept what we were spoon-fed, but instead, were searching for more than the mundane ritualistic attending church on Sundays. We were seeking something more substantial to hang onto. We wanted the spiritual part of our existence explored, to find a meaningful inner place within the religions that we practiced. Of course certain tenets and established criteria exist in all cultures, religious or not, and form the foundation of societal rules and boundaries. Yet, the spiritual seeker of this era recognized that these are the nuances of man and many of us were truly seeking a real connection to the Divine; a unification with the Spirit.

Thus, my generation was born into an era of change and embraced it as part of our existence on this earth. We were born to be the changers, the ones to bring spirituality to a higher realm. We fought within ourselves to find a place in this world for our souls to flourish as we questioned the authorities. It was the change around us that taught us that the only thing that is constant in life is change. The constant change in the world in which we grew to adults, defined a piece of who we are today. Many of us went through the process without giving it much thought, we followed the crowd. Some of us were brought to a higher understanding and shouted this from peaks and valleys to whoever was willing to listen and actually hear our voices. While still others were quiet in their comprehension of the life they witnessed around them. Yet, we had a lifetime in front of us. And, it takes a lifetime to learn and experience what the Spirit needs to teach.

Again life changed and mutated into peace, a peace that would last until September 11, 2001. During the 1970's peace was on the horizon and the country settled down and permitted the chaos of the 60's to be relegated to a painful memory. But the mindset of the people was altered permanently. They were now seeking the "meaning of life" and their own spirituality. My parents, who were always on the spiritual edge, (not only did they acknowledge my "sight" but they were having glimpses into the spirit realm as well) joined a movement called the "Catholic Charismatics." This movement promoted the healing Spirit of God via prayer groups, seminars and large evangelical events. We were still in the wake of the 60's; we were all still recovering and healing. This movement was a radical shift in the church toward accepting and communicating with the Holy Spirit. It incorporated speaking in the Spirit (speaking in tongues); seeing images and discerning the ability to just know the truth about others via Divine intervention (clairaudience). Countless charismatic prayer groups spread like wildfire across the country, especially on Long Island. This was a movement which expanded the traditional doctrine of the church and took spirituality to a higher level.

I am forever grateful that I was permitted to be a part of this movement and was able to witness the power of the Spirit through these prayer groups. This all gave credence to the gifts I already possessed and helped me on my path to ultimately accept these gifts as fruits of the Spirit. I was able to recognize my oddities as true gifts from God. I was in awe of the Power and the energy that moved through me and with me.

As time moved on, I spent my teenage years going to prayer groups and yearning for more. As a young girl I was praying with people and laying my hands on them imploring God to heal them. My intuitive center was increasing and intensifying and I began to "see" (clairvoyance) things about people. More and more people would ask for me to pray with them and lay my hands on them. Although I knew this was not the norm (my friends were not experiencing anything of the sort), it was a normal part of my life and that of my family. It was so special to me because I truly felt a community of love and the presence of the Spirit of God. It was also probably the only part of my life that I felt a sense of belonging and true acceptance without any ulterior purposes or motives on the part of others or myself. I began to recognize the feeling that preceded an image or an intuitive message and my eyes were open to a whole new world and way of living and viewing life.

Thus, as the many, many summers turned into winters and springs into falls, as my life changed and I grew into adulthood; with increased frequency I began to use and explore my innate Divine gifts. When I finally stepped into a place of pure acceptance and gratitude, I accepted these tributes from heaven and honored them. It was then that my fear disappeared and my gifts were unleashed, free to grow in leaps and bounds. The fear was replaced with a courage that was supported by the universe, so that I could stand up and say, "I am a healer." And so, I am.

~Two~

A Mere Woman in Suburbia

There never was a great soul that did not have some Divine inspiration.
Marcus T. Cicero

What truly is a modern day healer? There has been much hub in recent years concerning mediums or spiritual intuits; people who communicate with the spirit world. John Edward, Sylvia Brown, Vincent vonPragh, Allison DuBois are to some extent household names; their gift of communication with the other side widely accepted and respected. Yet, they are the famous few. They are the forerunners who paved the way; opened the door for others equally as gifted to have the courage to step out into the light with their own gifts. The other mediums, less renowned, may not be on television, the radio or for that matter, have their books or their names plastered on the sides of buses. Most mediums are regular, unassuming people whose names you probably have never heard. I am one of those people.

In most ways I am an average forty-something year old woman. Similar to many of you, I am a wife, mother, daughter and a friend. I have been President of our elementary school PTA; attend parent-teacher conferences; go to corporate events with my husband and play Bunco (a game that suburban housewives use as an excuse for an evening out!). I cook, clean, bake, and wipe away tears from my sons' faces. I, like everyone else at times, succumb to stress, anxiety and worry. I am highly educated in certain realms and rather ignorant in others. I transport children to baseball games, and soccer matches, attend school plays, cry at graduations and other milestones in my children's lives, lament about their future and agonize over losing them to the world. I plan with my husband for our tomorrows as we sit at our kitchen table, early in the morning, drinking coffee or orange juice. I have worked as a waitress, a salesperson and a business executive. I am an American woman.

However, in the midst of all this and, despite my busy life, I also have found the time to converse with those on the other side as I move through the daily routine of my life. These wonderful, beautiful souls enter my consciousness and speak to my heart. I hear them, feel them and allow them to spend time with me in the hope that I can somehow relate their messages to their loved ones. The purity of their actions is outstanding and incomprehensible. With chaste love they expend their energy and manifest themselves to me in order to help those who they will love forever. They have taught me that love goes on eternally as it is carried over to the world beyond. I also understand that there is no death, only a transformation of the body that we are. Although our physical bodies may turn to dust, our souls just move from one plain to another.

So, as I move through both the somewhat mundane routines and the exciting moments of my life, spirits from the other side grab my attention. Often it is when I am doing something mindless, almost robotic, that they find their way into my sphere. Intelligence is obviously another trait that follows into the next dimension since they cleverly make themselves known to me. As I maneuver the roast chicken into the oven and lose myself to the chopping of vegetables for the salad, my mind is clear and detached. This is when those on the other side perceive a way to get my attention. It is at these times that I am a clear channel. My mind is not engaged and I am going through a moving meditation of sorts. Thus, right in the middle of my kitchen, it is very common for me to be having a very animated conversation with a spirit.

Remember the movie "The Sixth Sense?" Great movie, but if I were that poor boy, I would be frightened out of my wits! He saw dead people, almost like zombies, in the state they were in when they died. If someone was killed by a blow to the head with a hatchet, the boy saw the hatchet still sticking out of the person's head with blood oozing everywhere. Yuk! The little boy in the movie also saw the walking dead right in front of him, just as we, the living, see each other. I have no doubt there are those that experience this and accept it. God gives you what you can handle. I do not think that I could handle that sort of visitation.

When I see and hear spirits, there is a large element of emotion and energy sensory at play. As an empathic intuitive, I am sensitive to the emotions that surround me and feel them in my own body. Therefore, as the spirits visit me, I feel the air around me change and the personality of the spirit comes through. Also, most times these feelings are accompanied by images, which appear in my head, or an unquestionable knowing (clairsentience). I may just know what the spirit looks like. It may seem strange to you, but it is even stranger to me! My mouth opens and out come physical descriptions of people I have never met.

Though, when I receive images they are usually for me, as the messenger or voice, to use to describe the spirit. These images may not be exactly what the person actually looked like while he or she was walking the earth, yet my description will include certain features or attributes that are relevant for their loved ones to recognize them and validate their presence. I may describe height and stature, ethnicity, texture and color of hair, hairstyle or prominent facial or other physical features. The spirits may show me a person who I actually knew in my life, who possessed similar physical characteristics, to help me describe them. For instance, I might be shown an old man who I knew as a child who had a big nose. I would relate the physical characteristics shown to me such as the height of this man, his age, his hair color, the size of his nose, or whatever physical attributes necessary for me to translate, and pass on the information.

However, it is the personalities of the spirits who come to me that make the greatest impact. It is the feeling of their personas, the essence of who they are, not their physical appearances that are prominent. Their appearances may have changed over the course of their lives, but their personalities have remained constant. Thus, it makes sense, that spirits are usually most recognizable by their personalities.

Whether I am in my kitchen or somewhere else alone, or sometimes in a group of people, I am not always aware to whom the message should be delivered. So, it is important for me to ask the spirits surrounding me. And, they tell me or they show me. And then, they pass on the messages. It is important for spirits to pass on some specific piece of information to validate the truth of their appearance. Sometimes, I physically feel where the pain was prior to their death, or receive specific messages or statements, which I could not know, yet the receiver of the information is well aware. Sometimes the receiver cannot validate all the information and must pass on the information to other members of the family for validation. It is such a good feeling when the connection is made. Again, every message I receive conveys a deep love; a love that is almost tangible. I can feel it in my own body.

Yet, this is not the only way that I receive these wonderful messages. Sometimes my own spirit guides connect with others in the spirit realm and are able to bring the messages across to me. This frequently happens when I am doing a group reading. There are usually so many spirits in the room that my guides filter the messages and sometimes present them to me. It is more of an all knowing, clairsentience, then actually hearing a voice, or seeing an image. My mouth just opens and out comes the most fantastic information. I do not think about it, it just flows from my mouth. It is so cool, even after all these years; I am perpetually moved by the encounters.

These encounters and visitations have been primarily for those who happen into my life. Sometimes I can turn these amazing souls away and sometimes they are very persistent and just need to be heard. I am their way to touch those they love. They somehow searched and found me. And, they know that I will pass the information on no matter how much of a lunatic I may seem to those receiving it. It is not for me to judge. I cannot deny this great gift that I possess. I choose to unwrap it and let the gift change my life. Therefore, I welcome these souls. They communicate with me in my car, in my kitchen, bedroom and in other people's houses. They have no preference. It is all about getting through. Sometimes their messages are clear and other times it requires a bit of deciphering. All in all, if they want to get through, they will. And they do.

Can you feel their message? Can you hear it? They have been prompting the writing of this book. They want you to know, that this is a real phenomenon. They want you to listen with your head, your heart and every one of your senses. It is all about being aware and opening up so that they can communicate with you. It is about accepting that life, in another form, goes on. It is the knowledge that, without question, your loved ones who have passed, are around you and want you to know that they love you and hear you. When you cry out in the middle of the night, "I love you!", or "I miss you", with deep yearning for them, they are hugging you and screaming back "I love you too, but I am here!" It is about when you look at your child and see in his or her face the reflection of someone else and feel profound joy; they are saying "It is me! I live on in the child! I am so proud!" When you close your eyes and you feel their presence, do not doubt it. Give them their due and acknowledge the feeling as truth.

You might be wondering how I went from "spiritual healing", in a pretty traditional sense, to carrying on conversations with those behind the veil. It did not happen all at once for me as it might happen for some mediums; it progressed over time and when I was ready to accept the expansion of my own existence into a reality that was not the ordinary, I finally gave in. It was when I said out loud to the heavens, "I am ready", that the real teaching began. I am perpetually the student and crave the teachings. The heavens, and my God, are well aware of this. They also know all my idiosyncrasies. Accepting these realities, I entered a spiritual classroom and progressed through each level methodically in a way that was comfortable for me.

As I mentioned previously, having always seen and felt spirits and angels around me, the gift was given to me yet I did not instantly completely unwrap it. I peeked in. Maybe undid the ribbons, but never took off the lid of the box. This gift was never even spoken about outside of my immediate family. Even worse, I learned how to push these spirits away for the better part of my life. Something had to jolt me; motivate me to want to bring these spirits through. And, when that something happened, I began to gradually allow myself to open my heart and communicate with those behind the veil. At that point, I began to step with Grace onto my path and to recognize the journey that was truly my life. Not being a patient person — expected to blossom into a super medium over night; but that was not to be my experience. The universe was far more astute and my gift developed at a slower pace than I initially desired. The universe sent healers, mediums and others who could lead me on my path. Many of these people saw something in me that was hidden deep within my soul and helped to bring it out. They helped alleviate my fears about stepping out and helped replace fear with a steadfast courage. Their words and their support made me brave, and gave me the fortitude to "walk the walk" and certainly "talk the talk" of a medium.

But I digress; you must be asking what prompted my change of heart? What was that something that altered my life? Well, everyone's life has dips and valleys. I had been ignoring my spiritual abilities in order to go through the motions of life. My ego was in control as college, marriage and work in the jungles of corporate America began to define my life. The carousel of life left me breathless. The spinning increased until I needed to get off the ride. I recognize now that I needed to be shaken — to be literally, brought to my knees to accept who and what I was born to be.

In order to fully comprehend the light and to live in it, many of us need to experience a deep dark void. The aloneness as our ego screams, "Only *you* can save *you*!" Of course, this is a lie. As many mystics have experienced, it is in entering the darkness that the light can truly be seen. The light is always there but sometimes the contrast is necessary for the soul to grow. Mystics speak of God piercing the darkness, arms outstretched, reaching into that deep black hole to pull them out into the rays of the sun; into the perfect union. This darkness is appropriately called "the dark night of the soul." St. John of the Cross, a prominent Catholic mystic and saint who coined the phrase "emerged from his dark night"; a time when he was literally locked in a cell, covered with lice and infection and escaped through God's Grace. John then began to unite with Divinity and encounter his own gifts. In a less dramatic way that was true for me as well.

During a dark period in my life, I felt the walls moving in on me — suffocating me and attempting to steal my very breath. I could not breathe and did not know which way to turn. I felt imprisoned and helpless. I turned to my God, and through my spirit guides and by virtue of my heart wrenching prayers, I began to naturally meditate. I was never taught meditation in the classic sense, but in retrospect, I was able to free my mind, clear the slate within and allow the universe to talk to me. I was divinely guided to this state. And in this state, as I tore off some of the wrappings, my gift was permitted to grow.

In my meditative state, I began to see the lives of people across the globe and feel their pain and their joy. I heard their prayers and was asked to pray for them specifically. And it was intriguing to me that I was, to some extent, able to verify their existences and their problems. My perspective on life changed.

It was as if, with scraped knees, I crawled out of the black night and emerged, back erect and reached for the sun. With arms up to the heavens, I have been reaching ever since. I had no choice but to accept who I was, the good, the bad and the ugly. Although I am scarred, I accept the Divine inside of me and trust my inner voice, the voice of my own intuition and that of my guides. At that time, this was a revelation so great to me, on both a conscious and soul level. As I climbed out of my prison, I shed my shield and replaced it with a candle, a beacon to the spirit world and to the human race. I was, and still remain, the lighthouse guiding souls on the other side back to shore, back home. For me, among the blessings of my family, this is my greatest gift. I am in awe of the "Powers that Be" in allowing, little me, to carry out such a great job. I am forever thankful and forever in awe at the beauty of life here and on the other side.

My sixth sense grew and matured slowly, but was really ready to blossom once I moved with my then young family to the foothills of Connecticut. It was at that time that my horizons expanded into the healing realm. I was constantly being exposed to and being taught different modalities addressing the metaphysical aspects of our existence. I attended seminars and learned to have an open mind, a much broader view of the world and the spirit realm. My soul was paving the way for me to truly be who I was born to be. And now, although I am still growing, I have learned that my gift of mediumship encompasses all that I have learned in my life. It is to help people heal; to bring comfort and solace and to close the wounds that were left gaping when someone passed on. My mission is to bring words of consolation and support from the other side and to ease the burdens of the living.

~Three~

Living with a Medium – What a Trip!

It is kind of fun to do the impossible.
Walt Disney

I can think of lots of activities to be involved in instead of cooking. I am not a terrible cook, but my family just likes to eat the same food. It gets a bit monotonous. When I try to spice it up, they balk. They are creatures of habit and are set in eating what is a proven success. When I gave up working out there in the real world, I promised to take over all the "household" tasks which include washing clothes, cleaning, being the chauffeur for the children and alas, cooking. Although I have gotten better, I did not even know how to cook until I moved to Connecticut and was married for fifteen years! Imagine that. Oh, well, now I am the resident chef, waitress and head of dishwashing services. This is a duty that does not get its fair share of kudos.

Anyway, I have learned that although these tasks may not be the highlight of my day or my life, they are mindless and allow my mind to rest and my perceptions, intuitions, my clairvoyance, clairaudience and all my other "clairs" to go into "receive mode." At that point while I am walking around the kitchen, or chopping away without really thinking, is when the sheer movement becomes a meditation. It is at that point that I can see, hear and feel those who are unseen to most. Those on the other side slip in when our minds are free from the clatter of our days and lives.

A few years ago, as my family relaxed in front of the television, I was in the kitchen working away, similar to a scientist concocting something in a laboratory. By the way, since I am perpetually watching my weight I do not eat any of the "delicious" meals I put together. This is a true blessing! Anyway, as I prepared the meal, cutting and dicing rhythmically, I felt a presence in the room. Without looking up, I take in the personality; allow all of my senses to engage and absorb the presence. I feel the personality as if it were tangible. The sense of "feeling a personality" is a big one for me. Everything about the person that I need as an introduction comes through this feeling. Like those that are living in the flesh, those on the other side are happy, sad, funny, depressed, anxious, serene, grouchy and feisty personalities. Their personalities mirror the personalities they had in life. How else could they be recognized? And, for me, it is their personalities that precede anything else.

On this particular day, I identified this personality as male, playful and funny. After the personality sets in my mind; an image of the person comes through. As previously mentioned, most times the spirit does not appear as the person looked while they walked the earth plain, but rather is similar in characteristics so that I can pass on those traits. I am only the messenger but it has to be an image that makes sense and is memorable to me. In this case, I saw a man that use to be an usher in church when I was a little girl. Although personality-wise, this man from my past and this spirit beside me were at odds, physically they were identical. The man from my youth, as well as the spirit, were around

5'8, had white hair and pleasant features. Both men commanded a presence despite their smallish stature.

"Okay," I said after I was confident of the personality, the image and my connection, "please tell me who you are and what you would like me to help you with."

"I am George. Talk to my daughter for me," he simply stated. "Tell Karen it is all okay and that I am with her; what she feels is really me. I know she thinks about me every year at this time."

Later, I learned it was the anniversary of his death. This was not known to me since I had not known Karen when her father had died. Moreover, he had passed on such a long time ago, that she did not discuss it. We were just casual friends at that point. However, George's visits initiated and helped develop a close friendship between Karen and me that has grown over the years.

George went on to tell me about specific events or referenced certain items that would allow Karen to accept that he had really come through. He spoke of a ruby ring that was her connection to him. I later found out that he had given her a ruby ring that she had not worn for years. You can bet she wears it now! After listening to him for about thirty minutes, I walked into the family room where my husband and sons were watching television. Standing in front of the room, I announced, "Karen's father was just talking with me in the kitchen."

My oldest son looked at my husband and said, "He must be dead."

That is it; that simple and they went right back to the program that they were watching on television. This is not a big deal, it's just mom doing her thing. How cool is that? They almost think that what I do is run-of-the-mill and normal. I am not saying that they do not think that I am strange, but what kid does not at some point think his or her mom is just plain weird? So I am defined as weird; there are worse things.

The experience with this particular spirit was enlightening to me as it continued to unfold over the next year with constant visits. George would come to me in my car, the grocery store, my laundry room, anywhere and any place he knew I would listen. I knew what his presence felt like so getting through to me and having me recognize his presence was easy. This spirit was intent on speaking to me on a daily basis and he would push into my existence to pass on some piece of information to different members of his family. George made them all believers in the afterlife. When he related an in-dept description of his wife, even her thoughts, and actually showed me, in detail, the room in which she sat at night, his family was amazed. George wanted his family and especially his wife to know that he was hearing them and answering. He also passed on information for his son and later for his son-in-law.

From what I have been told, these people would sit around the holiday table discussing the messages he passed onto me. They searched for holes in the stories; but could not find any. It gave them a sense of acceptance about his death and why he had to leave this world. George went into great detail about his life; the pain he experienced while on the earth and the reason he had to pass on when he did. His family was granted peace and understanding in knowing that he is happy and always with them.

George was quite a character in life as well as on the other side. It seems to me that he manipulated me into listening to him by so blatantly teaching me, in depth, how to tune in and out at my own will to the spirit world. He also taught me how to call forth spirits that were not standing in front of me. So, in the end, my teacher was a charming dead man! But, I listened; who better to teach me about the spirit world than a spirit. And, the protocol for me to connect; the ways and means for which I had been searching for years, were told to me over the period of about ten months. George was a wonderful teacher and helped me so very much. For that, I am eternally, and I mean eternally, grateful. What a guide he was! His tidbits to his family were sometimes heart wrenching and sometimes out of a comedy routine. He would even fight for the limelight with his mother, another strong spirit personality, only to acquiesce and give her the stage.

One of George's daughters felt very left out when he did not have any messages for her. When I asked George for a message for her, her paternal grandmother, George's mother pushed into my awareness. Obvious to me, she felt that this was her special granddaughter and that she was the one who rightfully should communicate with her. And so it was. In the end, everyone in the family was able to speak with someone on the other side through me. I cannot control who will speak with whom. I can only hope that whoever does appear will pass on a message that aids in our constant process of healing.

As the previous story indicates, my immediate family has become accustomed to the strange occurrences in our home as I go about my routine tasks. Yet, my entire extended family has not always been privy to my conversations with those on the other side. On the Tuesday morning before Thanksgiving, my husband was good enough to take my youngest son to school while my oldest son, who was ill, was still in bed. This left me two hours of "free time" (which was a much sought after commodity to me). At 7:10 a.m. on this morning, I decided to wrap some Christmas presents. I closed my bedroom door and in the silence of my room began the mindless task of robotically wrapping gifts. I find this task very relaxing as it presents me with time to ease my mind and drift into a meditative state. As I repeatedly cut the paper, folded it and taped it, my mind cleared and my channel was open. In the middle of the second gift, I knew I was not alone.

I felt a very lighthearted personality with me. The feeling overwhelmed me and made me giggle a bit. Then, in my minds eye, I saw a balding man, kind of like George Burns with sparse hair. An image of a person who looked to me like he occasionally enjoyed a good game of cards and a good cigar. The spirit world really taps into me so that I can relay messages. This particular lighthearted spirit seemed to play with me as he danced around my senses. Then in my mind, I heard him say that he was Brenda's father. I was confused. Brenda? I searched my brain. Who was Brenda? Then the only Brenda who I knew popped into my head; yet it seemed a long shot at best. The only Brenda I knew is the wife of one of my sister-in-law Linda's cousins. I saw this woman infrequently, for maybe fifteen minutes once a year or so. I knew very little about her except that her father had died some years ago (I had never met him), that her mother lived in Florida and her daughter was an athlete. I said out loud, "well, what I am supposed to do with this?" I heard a shout in my head "CALL LINDA." I thought to myself, *this is crazy*. I had never ventured out and had a conversation with an in-law about the subject of my conversations with those in the world beyond. I heard the shout again and I thought, *Okay, I will give this a try and risk them all thinking that I am nuts.*

I called Linda and implored her to ask Brenda if her father was bald, smoked a cigar, played cards occasionally and was a somewhat short man. Linda asked me to edify what I meant by short. Immediately, I heard, "I am 5 feet 8 inches!" Given the people involved, I wanted to slow this down a bit. I told her his height and tried to persuade her not to go out of her way or rush to call Brenda. I suggested that when she had a chance that day, if she wanted, she should give Brenda a call. Less than five minutes after Linda and I hung up, she called me back. She told me that Brenda's father was 5'8" and balding. At this point I felt I might be onto something and to avoid the telephone tag, I suggested that Brenda call me directly.

And so at 7:30 in the morning, Brenda called wondering what was going on. I told her that I had some messages from her father. Brenda's quickly asked, "Did you go to a medium?" Again, very few people knew about my communications with the spirit realm. I told her that her father was with me at that moment giving me messages to relay to her. I told her that he was very playful and that he wanted her to know that he was very happy. I felt the happiness. He conveyed that he is always with her. He told me that she had been looking too hard for him when he was standing at her side all along. She began to cry. I continued and asked Brenda if her father played cards and smoked a cigar occasionally. Brenda said she did not think so. I inquired if someone had been to the cemetery recently because he was acknowledging that someone had been there. She said that she was the only one who visited his grave and she had not been there for six months. Another piece of bad information. What was going on? I tried once more. "Did he really love the Thanksgiving holiday more than any other holiday?" Once again, she denied any knowledge. Oh well, I thought, I tried, maybe this was just something in my head. We hung up and I went back to wrapping.

However, this spirit was persistent and would not leave me. Although I was perfectly fine physically in the preceding moments, all of a sudden I began to get the heavy, bloated feeling of being constipated. This was too weird. A few minutes later the phone rang again. It was Brenda. She had called her mother who happened to be at her sister's house on Long Island. She had come in for the holiday.

Brenda told me that her mother confirmed everything that I had said. Her father had played cards occasionally,

43

smoked cigars, loved Thanksgiving best of all the holidays and, when her mother had come in from Florida the prior week, she had gone to the cemetery. Bingo! I now felt a bit of confidence in now passing on the next piece of information. I told Brenda about the feeling of constipation, thinking that it might have something to do with her father's illness before he died. Again she said that she just did not know how he felt. Okay, I thought, enough information, I need to start my day. We again hung up and I went to get some gas in my car before heading over to the hair salon to have my hair cut. While at the pump, I kept hearing the name Buster and the words "it is connected to a Jewish name." I called Linda and asked her what Brenda's father's name was. She said his name was Harry. I laughed at myself for now imaging information on my own; I thought I had heard him say the name "Buster", not Harry. But, he did not say whose name it was . . . Oh, well, I thought, I really have to get on with my day and let this go!

While sitting in the parking lot outside of the hair salon (I am always early for everything as you can well imagine. I was wrapping Christmas presents at Thanksgiving!), I checked my answering machine at home and heard Brenda's voice. I rang her back at once. She had called her mother again to help to validate the information passed on by me. Her mother told her that her father had a terrible case of constipation. This bout of constipation ultimately brought him to the doctor who diagnosed him with the stomach cancer which eventually took his life. I asked her about the name Buster. She told me that Harry's best friend was nicknamed Buster. I inquired about the Jewish name associated with this man and she told me that his real name was Abraham. Okay, the validations were pouring in and I was getting more and more excited to be passing on correct information.

Once again, I felt Harry telling me that he knew she was trying to connect with him and that there was some guilt associated with it. He wanted her to know that he was there with her. She should not always look for the larger than life messages from the other side but for the more subtle messages. Brenda told me that she was perpetually seeking him and that she had gone to a John Edward's gathering on Long Island hoping to be chosen by John and hear from her father. I suggested to her that her father's personality was probably not aggressive enough to come through in a large gathering of multitudes of stronger spirit personalities; or maybe it just was not the right time. He might have come through to me because he knew I could receive and that I would, with enough of a push or nagging, step out in faith and connect with her. She told me that she felt guilty for not having a private reading with John Edward but that it was very expensive and there were no guarantees.

"Well", I said, "Happy Thanksgiving and Merry Christmas, Brenda. This is your present from your Dad."

Harry told me to tell her that he would never leave her and that he loved her very much. He said he would be spending Thanksgiving with her and the rest of the family. At the end of what I thought was our last conversation, she told me that she would have paid anything for what came through that morning. At that point, I felt Harry's energy pull away. He had accomplished his goal.

However, the phone rang later that day. It was Brenda. She wanted to know whether or not her father had said anything about her sister. I said that I had imparted all the information given to me and the focus of the conversation was her and no one else. She said that her sister was very disappointed that her father did not mention her. Her sister had said, "Daddy always favored you." I told her that I only can say what comes through to me; this time the message was for her and only her. The spirits on the other side definitely have their own minds, motives and wills; all of which I cannot control. I do not know the reason that they do not come through for everyone in the family, but it is not my call, it is their choice. You cannot make everyone happy all the time. I wish that I could, but I am just the messenger.

I know this all sounds pretty incredible and impossible, but connecting to the spirit realm is probably the easiest feat I have been able to accomplish. Also, it is the most fun and certainly the most rewarding. To this day I am blown away by the specifics and the details that come through. It always makes me feel good when the recipient of the information says, "Wow, that is amazing that you are able to relate such specific details about someone that you never knew or of whom you never heard anyone speak." It feels real good to know that the spirit world is effectively communicating with me and that I am able to relay the information correctly. It is frightening to think I could be totally off base and subject to ridicule. But that is just my ego, which I try to push aside. I have to step out of my ego-self or I would never be able to put myself on the line and risk being ridiculed.

It is rewarding to demonstrate to others that the impossible is not so impossible. And it is more satisfying when the impossible becomes possible every day. Walt Disney had visions that he made come true. I think, just maybe, I can bring my visions to someone else so that they can live their lives more productively; establish their beliefs more broadly and be happy. That is my dream; my Disney World.

~Four~

Walking with the Angels

Angels descending, bring from above,
Echoes of mercy, whispers of love.
Fanny J. Crosby

Millions of spiritual creatures walk the earth
Unseen, both when we wake and when we
sleep.
John Milton, <u>Paradise Lost</u>

People are always asking me if intuitive gifts are genetic. Perhaps. I have not conducted any studies, nor have I thoroughly researched this topic. It is more important that the family support the emergence and growth of any and all gifts in their family members. If God dispenses gifts, unique to each one of us, and we sublimate these treasures, then we are unaware of the magnitude of the Power within us. If we can truly experience our gifts, and be supported by a family that welcomes our uniqueness, then we can grow into the people we were meant to be. However, if our gifts are ignored or dishonored when we are children but permitted to surface later in life, it may take a "reinvention of self" to accept and allow them to mature. It is unfortunate that this takes time and effort when it is a natural phenomenon that should be permitted growth and exploration beginning in childhood.

As I mentioned, I was fortunate that my gifts and the awareness of the spirit realm were not only accepted by my family but promoted by them. It was treated as very normal and natural. And so, logically, since I have always been consciously aware of angels, I thought that everyone saw them. I was rather surprised and sadden the day I learned that very few people *admit* to seeing them. What a shame to miss their soft yet powerful presences!

Angels are beautiful beings of light. I do not see winged creatures dressed in iridescent blue; rather just a soft white fluttering usually in the corners of rooms or hovering above or around people. They are rather direct beings in that they are who they are. If you ask a question, they seem to take it literally and give back a direct answer. Otherwise, they seem happy to just float and protect and bring light.

When they want to show us their presence they are capable of remarkable feats. I have a clear recollection of being about four years old and finding little unique "gifts" around the house – a tiny container of talcum power, a small box of candy, little innocuous, curious things. Of course my mother wanted to know where I found these little items since she had never seen them before in our house. I knew in the innocence of my child heart that the angels were leaving me gifts to let me know that they were near me and that they loved me. As young as I was, when I would touch these gifts, the feeling of excitement and love would overwhelm me. And, to this day, I remember these trinkets and still believe that they came from the celestial realm around me.

Growing up in a very small house had its advantages. Almost everything was visible from various standpoints in the house. I would often see flashes of bright sparkling white slowly gliding past me, like drifting clouds on a summer's day. This image was frequent and drifted from room to room. If I mentioned my vision to my parents, matter-of-factly they would say it was an angel passing me by. As it was, my mother also saw these wispy puffs of bright white moving around us. It was just a plain and simple truth accepted by my family. No elaboration, nothing more, nothing less. I accepted it as a basic truth.

Angels are not a new phenomenon. Celestial beings have been referenced in various holy texts for centuries. In fact, angels are mentioned over one hundred times in the Old Testament and one hundred sixty five times in the New Testament (Chafer, Systematic Theology, II, 3). Moreover, angels are not just affiliated with Judeo-Christian beliefs, but are also mentioned in the holy texts of other religions. The Buddhist equivalents of angels are divas, or celestial beings. Some schools of Buddhism also refer to angels as dharmapalas or dharma protectors. In Tibetan Buddhism, divas are sometimes considered to be enlightened beings. In the scriptures of the Koran, many passages indicate that the angels are a part of the heavenly realm.

The word angel in Greek, aggelos, and in Hebrew mal'ak, means "messenger." They act as the bearers of good news and of warnings in the Old and New Testaments of the Judeo-Christian Bible. Angels appeared to the prophets and Kings in the Old Testament, as well as to Mary, Joseph, Jesus and the disciples in the New Testament. In the Koran, in Surrah Fatir, angels are mentioned as messengers. "Praise be to Allah, the Bringer into Being of the heavens and earth, He Who made the angels messengers, with wings - two, three or four." Okay, so the greatest books of at least four different religions reference these wonderful creatures. All these scriptures refer to them as messengers and protectors. Therefore, plausibly, if angels visited the earth in ancient times, they would present themselves to us today.

Although many of us subscribe to religions whose bibles reference and speak of these wonderful creatures, we do not fully accept them and thus, do not recognize them when they appear to us. Are we not the same human race that has walked this planet for centuries? Why is it that the writers of the holy texts acknowledged and accepted the appearances and messages of the angels and yet, today, we push this idea aside? Why can we accept that it happened in ancient times but not now? If they appeared then, does it not stand to reason that in our world, which is subject to disasters and pain, that angels would also appear? They did not become absorbed by ancient chaos; rather they are here now and needed just as much as they were in eras gone by. We suffer ourselves when we do not acknowledge their presence and do not relish in their messages.

More than this, our expectations cloud our vision and make angels the creatures of fairy tales. We expect beautiful beings, dressed in shimmering white flowing gowns and surrounded in brilliant light to appear miraculously before us wings spanning the sky like the good witch in the Wizard of Oz. Yet, as it is written in Hebrews 13:1-2 "Let brotherly love continue. Do not neglect to show hospitality to strangers, for thereby some have entertained angels unawares." They do not always take the form that we are programmed to associate with them. Imagine this, angels may even take the form of humans! It's true. You may meet a person while shopping in the supermarket whom you have never met. She may smile at you and warm your heart, maybe pass on a word or two to ease your pain that particular day, and in a split second you may recognize her for what she is, an angel. It is a sense; the intuitive side of your heart that connects you to the compassion that is emitted from these entities. Others of us need to be "slapped in the face" so to speak. Even Paul upon being rescued from prison, does not fully believes that an angel was his guide. As written in the Acts of the Apostles 12:6-10:

The very night when Herod was about to bring him out, Peter was sleeping between two soldiers, bound with two chains, and sentries before the door were guarding the prison; and behold, an angel of the Lord appeared, and a light shone in the cell; and he struck Peter on the side and woke him, saying, "Get up quickly." And the chains fell off his hands. And the angel said to him, "Dress yourself and put on your sandals." And he did so. And he said to him, "Wrap your mantle around you and follow me." And he went out and followed him; he did not know that what was done by the angel was real, but thought he was seeing a vision. When they had passed the first and the second guard, they came to the iron gate leading into the city. It opened to them of its own accord, and they went out and passed on through one street; and immediately the angel left him.

Well that is pretty profound. Yet, where does that leave you and me? Sometimes the celestial beings appear in the same way; most times they are much more subtle. The angels have to work extra diligently to affect our awareness. Our job is to open our eyes and see, not just absorb the world. Once we embrace truly living with our eyes open, we open a doorway for this world of angels and spirits to walk into our consciousness. We have to listen with our hearts and not just our minds. We have to expect miracles on a daily basis and look for the messengers as subtle as they may be. And, we must listen to the innocence of our children, for often they are our teachers pointing us toward a greater understanding and awareness of ourselves.

In my case, as I left my childhood behind and moved into adulthood, just the responsibility of living changed my life. It happens to most of us. We live in a world that is fast moving and dictates much of our existence. I did not focus as much on the esoteric side or the spiritual side of myself. Of course the knowledge was always lurking in my soul and at the back of my mind, but my eyes had closed. The responsibility of being a wife, mother and working in the world trying to make ends meet had shifted my awareness. The universe was screaming for my attention, as I ignored it at every turn. And my husband, who was not brought up with the same spirituality or experiences as I, was also struggling to balance life. And so as a busy family with two working parents we concerned ourselves with getting by and trying to get ahead. Deep spiritual discussion did not make its way into our home. We went to church periodically and went through the motions, but nothing touched us. The light had gone out for me and I was floundering. But the universe is kind and compassionate and desired to reel me back in. And so it follows, that in Divine Wisdom, the universe captured my attention through my first born son; who has proven over and over again, along with his brother, to be my greatest mentors on this planet.

When Matthew was about two years old, he began to speak of angels. He was a very articulate child and spoke often of seeing an angel named "Michael" and hearing Michael speak to him in his head. Matthew often complained that Michael talked too much and would get in the way of his thoughts. My husband and I accepted this and although we did not promote it, we did not negate it either. Matthew was left to his own devices and feelings about "his angel." Frequently, adults would think that my child was strange or he would frighten some adults by the things he would relate.

Matthew described Michael as being a boy about his own age at the time, very bright and full of "good feelings." He said Michael made him feel special. What Matthew was experiencing was the overwhelming feeling of love that emanates from the celestial beings. Michael came to Matthew because Matthew accepted him and believed in what he was seeing and hearing. Matthew was open to the realm of heaven.

Moreover, in addition, I believe that Michael had another agenda. I needed to be brought back. I needed a banner waved in my face. This could be just the trick. My husband also needed to experience the workings of heaven. And so, through our child, heaven came to all of us.

As the years progressed, Matthew continued to see angels. He saw them until he was about seven or eight years old. He also gave great credence to the messages they brought to him. So it stands to reason that when Michael spoke to Matthew, no one was able to dissuade Matthew from what he heard.

And so it happened, when Matthew was four years old, my father, with whom Matthew was very close, had a massive heart attack and was rushed to the hospital and put into the intensive care unit. We were told that he was to remain in the unit for at least two weeks, probably longer, and that his situation was very grave. After my husband and I had come home from the hospital one night, Matthew met us at the front door. Without any preamble, he directly informed us that his "Pop-Pop" would be coming home on Thursday. Knowing this was an impossibility given my father's condition, we gently explained to Matthew that Pop-Pop would be in the hospital for a couple of weeks and suggested that we pray for him to come home. Matthew would hear none of this. He insisted that my father would be coming home on Thursday. We were concerned by Matthew's adamancy, since we did not want him to be disappointed when his grandfather did not come home. We were attempting to protect him from the pain. Matthew ignored our rationale.

Finally, after some back and forth on this issue, Matthew asked us if we had seen the angel in the driveway. "Didn't you see the bright light in the driveway when you pulled up? I saw it from my room. He was so bright. He was waiting for you."

Vinny and I looked at each other. Of course, we had not seen anything. Yet this did not dissuade our son. Matthew went on, "That was Michael. He told me that Pop-Pop is coming home on Thursday."

Matthew was steadfast in his belief. Knowing that we could not sway him, we told him we believed him and permitted him to continue to have faith in what he saw and heard. Well, as it turned out, to our amazement, my father was released from the hospital on Thursday, two weeks earlier than expected, in deference to everything Matthew had told us. When Matthew found out, he looked at us with the innocence of his age, and told us to thank Michael for the news. And so we did.

Now, think about this for a moment: What if we had told Matthew that he should not make up stories? What if we dismissed the idea of angels? Not only would that have stunted his spiritual growth but our growth, and the growth of so many others who have heard this story over the years. To know that my child was in the presence of angels and felt no fear and only acceptance was a genuine gift to me. Given that, it should have yanked me back into my deep sense of spirituality. It should have opened my eyes and my awareness. I recognized the Grace given to my son; I understood it and respected it, but I did not enter into the realm for which I was being called. It took sickness and the pain of infertility, to bring me one step closer to the light. Alas, we are all fallible in our humanness.

At this point, you may be asking what the difference is between angels and spirit guides. I am no expert; nor is any living person. Everyone has their own opinion. And it is just that - opinion. There is no solid proof. I have read many different views on this subject; the opinions range from those who feel that angels and spirit guides are one in the same; while others, like me, see a difference. When I see and feel messengers from the angelic realm, the feeling is soft, full of compassion and love, but usually very subtle. When I see them, they are usually in the corners of the room, near the ceiling, hovering over someone or circling over a group of people. The Arc Angels come through with more power and are larger than life. They convey a sense of strong protection, especially Michael.

Angels do not belong to any one person. We all share the angelic realm but are each born with our own guardian angel, who remains with us for the whole of our life. This guardian angel belongs to you and you alone. It is your friend, your mentor and your protector in times of need.

There is a humorous commercial on television that depicts a woman going about her day with her guardian angel by her side. Although the guardian angel is present, he is preoccupied and really not paying full attention to his charge. So, with this lack of angelic protection, the woman falls and is subject to disasters. It is a funny advertisement, but the overwhelming truth of the message is that our angels do protect us.

All in all, angels are pleasant and instill a feeling of innate security and comfort. They are ancient creatures and have been circling and protecting human-kind from the beginning of time. I believe that they never walked the earth in the form that you and I are in, but rather have always help humans from above. They were created to help us and bring heaven to earth. They are the messengers and the carriers of God's wisdom. They may take the form of a human to help, but it is not a form that they remain in when the moment passes. As I mentioned, guardian angels remain with their charges, but are not their spirit guides. As celestial beings, angels do not have the fluid gift of communication that our spirit guides possess. When communicating with the angels you must be clear as to your intent, your questions and your ideas. Do not leave room for interpretation.

A great exercise to practice is automatic writing with your angels. Take out a pad and pen, sit in a quiet spot and write "Dear Angel" followed by a question for your angels that cannot be answered with a "yes" or "no." For instance, you may ask "what should I be doing with my life?" Wait a few minutes and then write down whatever comes to your mind; even if it appears to be silly. The answer that comes through is usually direct and to the point. You angel might say, "Exactly what you are doing now!" Or "You should be taking a class in social work. Stop delaying." Again, very direct.

On the other hand, spirit guides, in my view, are very different. First of all, spirit guides can come in many forms. The Native American Indians believed that we all have animal guides, or totem animals that protect us and teach us our whole lives. These were animals, who at one time walked the earth. They also are symbolic in their species of what we need in our lives. One theme usually carries us through our whole lives while others come and go, as we need them. Although we have many lessons to learn, the theme and the criteria under which we learn is constant. So, back to the Sheep Dog that appeared to me as a toddler. He gave me a sense of protection that I needed at that time in my life and provided unconditional love and security. He allowed me to ride on his back, symbolically, into the wilds of my imagination and psychic ability. To this day, dogs are my animal totems.

However, animals are not the only spirit guides. Spirit guides can also be in the form of humans who, like animal guides, have walked this earth at one time or another. Some guides share some of their time with many people and others just belong to you. In my case, I feel a great attachment to the Catholic mystic, healer and Cappuccin Italian priest Padre Pio. I have smelled his sweet perfume for over thirty years now. It took many years for me to figure out it was his perfume, but once I recognized it as such, I knew it to be true. I have felt his presence very strongly at certain points in my life and have seen him present with me. When I visited his church in San Giovanni Rotundo recently, I felt an overwhelming sense of communion with his spirit. I recognize that he does not just belong to me, others have witnessed his spirit and felt his power; yet I know, he helps me with my healing and leads me on my way. He is one of the many guides that help me in my practice and in my life.

A few years ago, I took a class in shamanic journeying. In shamanic practice it is believed that the soul is free to leave the body. When a person journeys, the soul leaves the body, and may travel to a spiritual aspect of places on the earth, or may go within the earth, or above. Many times during a journey the spirit guide introduces him or herself. The journey is fascinating. When I journeyed, I met my spirit guide in the upper world. He told me that his name was O'ka and that he was an Egyptian priest. His name meant nothing to me, but being who I am, I looked up the meaning of the name on the internet and found that it loosely means spirit guide! Coincidence? Not in my world! Now that I can put a name and face to my guide, communication with him is far easier.

Unlike our angel friends, spirit guides have a true gift of communication. They can speak allegorically, directly through speech, or affect our other senses depending upon how we, as individuals, best receive information from them. Spirit guides can be funny or serious. They were people once so they possess the traits of their humanness. And they speak when they deem it appropriate. I hear O'ka speaking to me, as well my other guides, at various times during the day. I do not have to be meditating or praying, and certainly not in a trance (now how would that look at a meeting with my son's fifth grade teacher? Not good!). I just hear them. Their voices are different than the voice of my conscience or my imagination. Of course, my imagination plays into it. Without imagination we are one dimensional and cardboard.

Imagination is not a bad word. It is the part of our brain that allows us to freely enter into worlds in which we are free to believe. It opens up our mind to new places and the spirit world. This is sometimes the venue through which our guides find their way in. I am keenly aware of when my imagination moves over for the reality of heaven in my presence. It is an all knowing, a feeling. Imagination may open the door, but then steps aside.

Back to the difference between angels and spirit guides. Spirit guides were living, breathing people or animals at one time. Those who believe in reincarnation will attest that their connection is that they have shared lives with their guides and their guides know everything about them. Others feel that these guides come through without full knowledge of the person, to learn about the person and help them as they go about their lives. Like the angels, they are there to help and protect but also to teach and lead. If you would like to meet your spirit guide, simply meditate and talk to him/her. Listen very closely and you will hear a voice answering you. Have a pad by your side and be ready to write. You might get an image or a feeling of who your guide is or you might hear him/her. Take whatever you receive and write it down on your pad.

So there you have it from my perspective. Again, we are all born with the "sight" to see our guides, whether they are angels or spirit guides. If you can allow yourself to move out of your social and tribal constrains and embrace your truth, you will experience the Truth of the heavenly realm. If you allow your children to go forward and believe what they see and reinforce their beliefs they can change the world. If my definitions work for you, that is terrific, hold onto to them. If not, that is okay. I hope they lead you to think about what it is that you believe and form your own beliefs. You are your own guru.

~Five~

There are No Coincidences

Learn to get in touch with the silence inside yourself and know that everything in life has a purpose. There are no mistakes, no coincidences, all events are blessings given to us to learn from.
Elizabeth Kubler-Ross

As I mentioned at the beginning, for some reason you were drawn to this book. Why? I do not know. You may not even know. But I do know this; there are no coincidences. To believe in coincidences ascribes to the belief of randomness in life; life as a component of nothing more than arbitrary circumstances. When something is placed before you, you have the choice, the free will, to embrace the event, the situation, the person or whatever it may be, or to walk away. Yet, the appearance of the event is by no means a coincidence. When you open your awareness and accept this as fact, it is amazing how coincidences turn into synchronicities.

Synchronicity is the experience of two or more events which occur in a meaningful manner, but are causally unrelated. In order to be synchronistic, the events must be related to one another temporally, and the chance that they would occur together by random chance must be very small. Synchronicities are people, places or events that your soul attracts into your life to help you evolve to higher consciousness or to place emphasis on something going on in your life. The more consciously aware you become of how your soul manifests, the higher your frequency becomes and the faster you manifest positively. Each day your life encounters meaningful coincidences; synchronicities that you have attracted.

Bear with me for a moment as I lead you into the world of academia. Synchronicity, a word coined by Carl Jung (1875-1961) a Swiss psychiatrist and a colleague of Sigmund Freud, is defined by Jung as an explanatory or clarifying principle. According to Jung, synchronicity explains "meaningful coincidences." In <u>The Structure and Dynamics of the Psyche</u>, Jung describes how, during his research into the phenomenon of the collective unconscious, he began to observe coincidences that were connected in such a meaningful way that their occurrence seemed to defy the calculations of probability. Following is an excerpt from the book in which Jung relates an incident that transpired while treating a patient:

> A young woman I was treating had, at a critical moment, a dream in which she was given a golden scarab. While she was telling me this dream I sat with my back to the closed window. Suddenly I heard a noise behind me, like a gentle tapping. I turned round and saw a flying insect knocking against the window-pane from outside. I opened the window and caught the creature in the air as it flew in. It was the nearest analogy to the golden scarab that one finds in our latitudes, a

scarabaeid beetle, the common rose-chafer (Cetoaia urata) which contrary to its usual habits had evidently felt an urge to get into a dark room at this particular moment. I must admit that nothing like it ever happened to me before or since, and that the dream of the patient has remained unique in my experience.

Have you ever seen a real life scarab? I certainly have not. Moreover, do your dreams manifest into reality? If so, do you think that it is by utter coincidence? Synchronicity is knocking on doors in the lives of average people every day. We just require the awareness to actually see and accept it at work.

Lately, I am devoting much time and effort to the women's retreats that I hold once a year. Every year it is important to get different speakers, "new blood" so to speak, to conduct workshops and seminars. Well, that is easier said then done while living in a somewhat remote area of the country. That being said, I do tend to use the internet to communicate with people all over the country and the world. And my address book is rather large. So, one day, I decided to send out an email (to clean up my address book) – inquiring as to who wanted to remain on my list and who wanted to be taken off.

Promptly, I received an email reply from a woman who I had never met and I had no recollection of our connection. She emailed me back explaining that she had never met me nor had she ever heard my name but felt a bond between us. She explained her work as a shamanic healer and suggested some ways that I might have gotten her email address. Nothing rang true to me at that moment, but I was intrigued by her reaching out to connect with me. And, since I do not believe in coincidences and wanted to find out the reason behind our fated connection, I spoke with her via email, telephone and finally in person. Initially, I recognized the impact she would have on the upcoming retreat. I knew that her contribution to it would be monumental. What I did not see was that she would be instrumental in my own healing. Is this all a coincidence? Believe what you will, but I think not.

Furthermore, coincidences come in many shapes and sizes. And, it is astounding how the universe and God has a way of bringing us back when we stray from our paths. We often forget where we are going; we just keep moving and going about our lives. We frequently wind up in a place that is not where we should be. Life goes 'round and 'round and so do we. Sometimes we just need to step off the carousel. It is when we step off for one moment, one nano second, that we experience the greatest "coincidences" imaginable. Unfortunately, often it is pain that makes us stop the ride. It is when we are going through great pain, either physical or emotional and have nowhere else to turn, that something, some "coincidence" happens and we become aware that we need help. It happens to all of us. It has happened to me.

When Matthew was two years old, we decided to try to conceive another baby. This proved to be a very challenging period in my life when conception just wouldn't happen for us. I raced from doctor to doctor attempting to determine a course of action. Yes, I have an abnormal uterus, but I had conceived and delivered Matthew without any problems whatsoever. Thus, I became obsessed with having another child. It is all I thought of; it consumed me and the pain of not being able to conceive was like a knife jabbing my consciousness at every interval. It hurt. People, in their desire to help, would unknowingly turn the knife as it dug deeper and deeper, increasing my pain. Conversations to ease my pain only intensified the reality of not getting pregnant.

A friend of mine, Vicky, who at the time was the mother of four beautiful, healthy children, all under the age of five years old, all conceived without a thought, professed to me that my problem was that I was not relaxed enough. I recognized that she desired to say something that would help me, but this comment and similar ones, only increased the emotional pain and were making me resentful and depressed. Although I knew that I was fortunate to have one healthy child, in my humanness, as my ego was permitted to explode, I wanted what I thought was best for me, and my family. I could not see beyond the pain. At that particular point in my life, it was as though a coma had taken over me. I was breathing and living by simply going through the motions of life. Indeed, I needed something to pierce my soul. I needed to be woken up with a jolt.

And so it went, that by the time Matthew was only months away from his sixth birthday, we still could not see another child on the horizon. It broke my heart when Matthew, in all his bravado, with his belief in angels close to his heart, told anyone who would listen, that his angel said we would be giving him a brother very soon. Knowing what I knew, I discounted his discourses and tried to tell him that sometimes families are just three people. He insisted that whatever his angel told him was true. And thus armed with the words of Michael as told to me via Matthew, I found hope to which I could cling.

I located a doctor who suspected that there was scar tissue in my uterus which might be blocking conception. He suggested that this tissue could be removed through a simple surgical procedure. A laparoscope would be inserted through my belly button into my uterus for a full view of the interior of this organ. If scar tissue was detected it would be removed which would pave the way for a conception. It appeared to me to be pretty simple and straightforward. If this procedure would allow me to conceive, I was right there and ready to move forward. This was a ray of light in my gloomy night. My doctor had given me something to hold onto and I pushed to have the procedure done as soon as possible. Unfortunately, the wait for an operating room at the major

New York hospital where Dr. Goldman belonged would be two months. And so I waited.

As I crossed the days off the calendar, Dr. Goldman telephoned me to let me know that his partner Dr. Redman would be performing the procedure. Finally, the day was approaching and I was looking forward to moving ahead. A few days before the scheduled date of the laparoscopy, I received a call from Dr. Redman.

"Anna, I have been giving your situation a lot of thought. Given the abnormality of your uterus, I do not feel like I am the right person to be doing this procedure on you."

I was stunned! What did she mean? I had waited two months and the date was finally here. This was my last thread of hope. The piece of flimsy cotton I had been holding onto for dear life was tearing; I was falling. What would I do? She recommended a fertility doctor, with whom I got in touch immediately and was able to secure an appointment, due to a cancellation, for later that afternoon.

Dr. Wayne, the fertility specialist, was a compassionate and very kind man. He advised me to consider a new medical procedure to remove the scar tissue. Ever the optimist, I latched onto this sliver of hope. Once again, however tenuous, hope threw me a golden rope and I had something to hang onto. He asked me to return on Monday, with my husband, for an examination and a detailed explanation of the procedure.

With Dr. Wayne's reassuring words buoying me through the weekend, my husband and I showed up at his office for our appointment. He was thorough in his examination and explanation of the procedure. Although he determined that I had cystic breasts, just an aside diagnosis, I was accepted as a candidate for the procedure. Vinny and I were excited. We had renewed hope and faith. Yet, we also decided that since the age gap between Matthew and the next child was widening by the second, if I was not pregnant in the next six months, we would be resigned to have one healthy beautiful child.

When I returned to work the next day and was relating the past week's events to one of my co-workers, Amy, I added that the doctor had told me that I have cystic breasts.

Amy looked at me and smiled. "Anna you are pregnant. That is a sign of pregnancy."

"Amy, you do not understand," I patiently explained, "I cannot conceive because of the scar tissue in my uterus."

She shook her head and laughed, "I would bet anything that you are pregnant."

Although I thought that she was wrong; I still had a shred of hope, that maybe, I could conceive on my own. In all the motions of going to doctors, scheduling surgery and running here and there, I had lost my focus. At this point, the idea that I might be pregnant had not occurred to me. During lunch time that day, I walked to a pharmacy and bought a pregnancy test kit. And so it came to pass, that it was in a stall in the ladies' room of my office, that I first found out that I was indeed going to have another child. I was in shock. To me this was nothing short of miraculous. And more so, the true blessing was the abrupt cancellation of the initial procedure, which would have harmed the baby. Was this a coincidence? I think not. The universe was screaming "Open your eyes!"

From the beginning, Joseph was a contender. He defied all odds in his grand entrance into this world. I had developed a pregnancy tumor that was competing with the baby and, as a result, was constantly bleeding. My doctors told me at every weekly visit, that I ran a high risk of losing my baby. Yet, I knew in my heart nothing in heaven or earth could block the emergence of my son onto this planet. In my sixth month, I began to have labor pains and my cervix began to dilate. I was admitted to the hospital, hooked up to intravenous with a betamethazone drip and given tribunal injections daily to postpone the contractions and ultimate birth of my baby. I was committed to total bed rest. To aid in holding the baby in my uterus, the bed was inverted at a forty-five degree angle. So every night with the blood rushing to my head, giving me a dull throbbing headache, the labor pains returned. And, since the baby was so large for his gestational age, on a daily basis, blood was drawn from my arms to ascertain that I did not have gestational diabetes. It baffled the medical staff that this baby could be so big at that point in my pregnancy. Given all of this, my doctor would counsel me about the high probability that the baby would not survive. In my heart of hearts, I knew that my baby was a miracle and would defy the odds. Of course, my unwavering belief that my baby with healthy, concerned the hospital staff who sent in social workers to discuss the probability of facing the dire circumstances if I was wrong.

Finally, eleven weeks early, Joseph pushed his way into this world and made his grand debut. He weighed a whopping four pounds eight ounces and was seventeen inches in length. On its face, this appears to be a low birth weight, yet it is common that babies born almost three months premature usually weight about two pounds. My baby was not only a substantial weight, but because of the steroids that were fed to me intravenously, he did not have to spend any time on a respirator, which would have posed a risk to his eyesight. Also, to the pediatricians' surprise and delight, Joseph was thriving and was released from the hospital after staying only four weeks. They called him the "miracle baby."

Joseph was a tiny little person when we took him home to meet his brother. He weighed four pounds five ounces when he arrived at his new home, but by the time he was three months old, he was a healthy fourteen pounds. We gave him Michael as his middle name in homage of Matthew's angel who so loving gave us the fortitude to continue on with our quest for Joseph. Today, Joseph is a healthy, happy little boy. He is a wise little man who has had a tremendous impact on our family. He is practical, sweet, forgiving and beyond all else, has a deep capacity to love and accept us all for who we are. He provides the stability that we have required over the years.

In retrospect, I recognize that I was being called to focus on the miracles around me and to get back on the track where I belonged. I had to refocus and pay attention to the synchronicities in my life. As my life moves from minute-to-minute and day-to-day, it is proven over and over again, there are no coincidences. Upon accepting this, my life has become much more fruitful and in tune with God and the heavenly realm. My suggestion is to live with your eyes open, recognize the synchronicities and accept that there are no coincidences. Be awake and present and the heavens will unfold at your feet.

~Six~

Who is this Person Interrupting my Prayers?

If we could all hear one another's prayers,
God might be relieved of some of his burdens.
Ashleigh Brilliant

I have found that the universe allows us to help each other when we least expect it; even when we are desperately attempting to help ourselves. A little flicker of light shines through for someone else, and our problems take a new perspective. During the time when I was spending hours meditating and praying for my sanity and well-being, I began to see visions of the life of another person across the globe. It was as though each time I entered a deep meditation another chapter of this person's life was exposed to me. Over the course of one year, I was emerged in the problems that affected this unknown person. At first, this annoyed me. I could not shake these visions. I did not understand. I wanted insights and guidance about my own life. I asked God to let me know the reason I was privy to this stranger's life and problems when, to me, it was clear that I needed the help. Everyone values their problems as monumental; I am no different. I tried to push away these visions at first, but I just could not. Like a boomerang they would come shooting back at me with a greater force. After a while, I recognized that the only way to rid myself of these visions was to accept them. Little did I know that these visions, the life of this man, this stranger across the oceans, would envelop so much of my own life. And so it passed, that for one year the viewing of this stranger's life helped to transform me and opened another window in my soul.

I saw, in my mind's eye, a man dressed in the garb of a priest or monk in an underground church in the Soviet Republic, which was in existence at the time of this experience. I knew it was the Soviet Republic because the symbols that stood for the USSR were shown to me. Frequently the priest was in his church, which was dark and very medieval looking. There were large cast iron lanterns hung from pillars on the sides which cast dim shadows across a brown stone floor. I knew it was not a vision of the past but rather the present day due to the clothing I saw the worshippers wearing. The overwhelming feeling of oppression and sadness was almost tangible and hung like a cloud within the confines of this holy building. Although I never actually heard the priest speak, I knew what he was thinking and the courage and fortitude that made up his persona. As the days turned into months, I witnessed via telepathy the imprisonment of the priest for his actions — for propagating his religion and fighting for religious freedom. I witnessed him writing letters while he sat in a dank, dark cell. He was lonely, but not afraid. I felt he had more to give the world and worried for his safety. It was shown to me that his name was J-o-s-e-f. The spelling of the name and not the articulation of it appeared somewhere behind my eyes. Each and every time Josef appeared to me, the words "Pray for him" were being screamed in my ears. So, not only did I pray, but I also enlisted my family to pray.

As fate would have it, one day, the visions stopped. Although I never found out for certain whom this priest was, ten years after the visions ceased I came across an article on the internet that validated the name of the person in my visions. The article spoke about Josef and described what I saw. Do I know for sure, if it was that particular man? I do not. It does not matter. The universe wanted me to pray and so I did. Sometimes a simple prayer is all that is needed. It was just one more lesson.

In retrospect, it is clear that heaven knew that I was praying unceasingly with a pure heart. My heart prayed as well as every cell in my body. So, the universe saw a way to capitalize on these prayers and refocus, at least some of my prayers, onto a poor soul who was in desperate need of help. Was it the angels, spirits or God Himself who moved me to pray for Josef? I do not know, and really it does not matter. Josef needed prayers and the power of prayer is enormous.

Thus, the power of prayer, spoken through a sincere heart, resides in God and not us. The power of prayer is not the result of the person praying. Rather, the power resides in God. 1 John 5:14-15 tells us, "This is the confidence we have in approaching God: that if we ask anything according to His will, He hears us. And if we know that He hears us - whatever we ask - we know that we have what we asked of Him." But, in the vein of my story, this may seem ridiculous. Why would God, who in the vast intelligence of the universe promote and permit visions of a complete stranger to come through to a person on the other side of the globe? Moreover, I am sure this priest and his congregation were praying for him diligently. Why was it so important that I had to pray? Why did I have to see this desperate but good man imprisoned for his convictions and a mission that was ultimately beneficial to the world at large? You may be pondering, as I did, these same questions. Well, I did not get it at first. I am a bit dense at times and need answers written in gigantic letters in the sky as well as banners to float slowly across my field of vision spelling out the answers.

Yet, when I got it; I really understood the magnitude of the Divine.

The universe operates so that we are all involved in healing each other and helping each other carry out our duties of love. By prompting me to pray, it not only helped Josef but also expanded my heart. My compassion for Josef grew in leaps in bounds and I longed for his safety and the continuance of his ministry. Not only was I bonded closer to God, but also to my fellow human being; someone I did not even know personally but grew to care about very deeply. Someone, who through this experience, and without even knowing it, had a tremendous impact on my life. I learned to cope with my own life through prayer. I was given more courage by viewing Josef's life. All in all, it was a phenomenal experience for me and another lesson on life, love and our interconnectedness. It also showed me how cool God can be when He decides to rattle and shake us. He really does know what He is doing.

~Seven~

Hey, are you Listening?

Listening is an attitude of the heart, a genuine desire to be with another which both attracts and heals.
J. Isham

I have been asked over and over again why those on the other side are still making contact and communicating with us. I think sometimes they just want to say "hi" or just let their loved ones know that death is not the end of love. Love continues and they are there to help and support from the other side. Sometimes, they may want to apologize for the wrongs that they did in their lives. Whatever the reason for their communication, they do come through with the personalities that they possessed in life – good or not so good. And, sometimes we want to hear from them and sometimes we just do not. And so it was with Donna. She did not want to hear from her father-in-law who was not a nice guy during his lifetime. But, as I say over and over again, we are not always permitted the choice in who comes through. If they can make their way through, we should just listen and do with it what we will.

The morning before Donna's healing session, I kept hearing a spirit's insistent voice ringing loudly. Then I saw an older man literally yelling "Dan" at me. That is all I saw and all I heard over and over again. Yes, they can be extremely annoying when they want to be! When Donna arrived, I recognized that I just could not do the healing session for which she was scheduled while Dan was at my shoulder. I thought, maybe, just maybe, she would receive some sort of healing through the connection with this man whoever he is. When I described to her what was going on and the persistent nature of this man, she indicated that her father-in-law's name was Dan. Similar to the workings of other spirits, once she validated the connection, Dan rushed in to show me something that would further authenticate his presence. He showed me an image of his big, bulky black laced shoes as I heard, loud and clear, the sound of the shoes as they noisily pounded wooden steps as he clumped up and down. Donna laughed and said it was true; they always knew when Dan came home.

Then, taking even me by surprise, having established his connection, he switched gears. Dan went on to say that he was truly sorry for the way in which he treated his kind-hearted wife. He explained to me that he had cheated on her during their marriage, and instead of being happy that she forgave him, he became angry. He felt unworthy of her love and felt guilty. Thus, although he loved her, he treated her terribly until the day she died. He revealed how his behavior detrimentally affected his children.

As Dan went on, I could sense that Donna was becoming agitated.

"Why is he coming to me?" she implored.

Dan answered that Donna needed to help his family and her husband, his son, come to terms with all of this and to reunite his family. At this, Donna became rather annoyed saying that she did not like Dan and felt that, as in life, he was once again, trying to manipulate the situation. She began to argue with him, through me. Well, this is not fun at all. It was very tough on me since I am only the messenger and before me stood this woman seemingly rather angry with me! Yet, I knew part of her healing was moving through the anger for herself and for her husband. She hurt for her husband and his mother and carried this anger with her.

As she argued with him, Dan did indeed manipulate the conversation and transgressed to her son, Henry. He told her how much he loved Henry and described a specific time and place when he was with him in spirit that Donna could verify. By changing the focus to her son and indicating that he was with him, Donna softened. By the time that Dan was ready to break his connection with us, Donna said she would try to help her husband come together with his siblings. Of course, that was not my plan for the hour or two I had put aside for her placid healing session, but it was what she needed at that point in time. She came to me to heal and so she did; just not in the way we had planned.

The spirit world is awe inspiring. The way in which they come through, though, is not always welcome. Sometimes they leap their boundaries when they have to communicate – like petulant children. And, being human, there are times when I am not too happy about them interrupting my life. As I mentioned in the beginning of this book, I am a suburban housewife living my suburban life. That being said, I like getting out with the girls once a month to play Bunco. Bunco is a simple game, probably created by a group of women who just needed an excuse to get out of the house periodically and chit chat. My older son and his friends have come to the conclusion that it is just a way for their mothers to find out what every kid in the town is doing – good and bad – and to hang around, sip wine and eat. They are not so far off from the truth. But in my case, although I think the chit chatting is fun, I really love to win. To me, even if its one dollar, winning is a definite goal. I am truly a competitive wench by nature.

So, now that you have a slight glimpse into my competitiveness, you will appreciate my frustration when one night last year, my game was interrupted by a spirit. I was happily playing Bunco at the house of woman I had met once in passing. Unlike games in the past where I was always the "biggest loser", on this particular night I was winning big time. I was childlike in my excitement. So there I was, rolling my dice to my little heart's content, when the hostess, Jane, approached me and asked if I felt anything or anyone in her house. At first, so lost was I in my game, the meaning of her question did not make sense. This was not in the context of me winning! I must have looked at her like she was a Martian! Clearly brushing her away, I told her that she had very nice energy in her house and dismissed the conversation by turning back to the rolling of the dice. In retrospect, this probably was not very nice, but I was winning! No excuse, I know. It did not matter; Jane was not going anywhere anytime soon. She continued to talk and ask me questions, clearly in pain and searching.

"I have heard so much about you. I thought maybe you would be able to see someone here." She was almost pleading to me.

Not to be rude, but also not to have my game interrupted, I told her that since I was playing a game and leading my own life at the moment, the spirits were respectfully standing at bay and letting me enjoy myself. Yet, she was not going to be set aside that easily. I later found out that she was previously employed as a stock trader. What a surprise; those people never give up! And so, Jane continued to stand at my shoulder imploring me to say something of relevance to ease her pain. Finally, when I realized that if I did not connect for her, I might lose the game, I asked whomever she needed to connect with to come through and, temporarily, or so I thought, stopped playing Bunco.

In a heartbeat, a beautiful blond woman appeared to me. She told me she had died of a particular kind of cancer and that she was in her thirties. She showed me her deathbed and indicated that she and Jane were great friends. She gave me some specifics about their friendship including the description of a piece of jewelry that her friends wore in commemoration of her. She went on to show me the children she left on this earth plain. I described all of this to Jane, thinking we were finished. But, this spirit went further; she described her husband's drug addiction and was begging me to relate the need for her mother to fight for custody of the children. She was particularly worried about the middle child. She explained the reason for her concern very specifically. By this point, Jane was hysterical. To say the least, because of all the drama, Bunco was over!! Can you believe that? I was the unofficial winner, who compassionately stopped playing to help someone, and I was not even given my winnings! Suburban women are tough and callous!

On a more serious note, this spirit pushed Jane to push me because the love she had for her children was more important than my Bunco game or for that matter anything else. No, I do not mean that exactly. What I really mean, is that the love she had for her children was not a "had", but a "has." Because their home environment was lacking structure as well as parental support and authority, and her husband was an addict, she had to reach out from the other side to help her young children. I was the portal through which she connected with her friend, who in turn, spoke with her mother and the custody battle went into motion. In the end I was thrilled to be a part of the salvation of these little children and showing once more that love never dies but continues from the other side of the veil.

~Eight~

Here I am, in the Zone

I felt as though I was driving in a tunnel. I had reached such a high level of concentration that it was as if the car and I had become one.
Arton Senna, F1 Race Car Driver

What happens when the spirits spontaneously push aside my everyday life and want to talk? There is definitely a modus operandi at play during these times. I frequently enter a "zone" where my pulse seems to slow, yet, I am keenly aware of the beating of my heart. A sense of elation fills my being; time stands still and my focus is intense and unwavering. I feel as though I am in a tunnel as calmness comes over me and everything in the room is blocked from my vision and perception, except the person for whom the communication from beyond is directed. Although I am conscious of my surroundings, I feel as though I am in an altered state of consciousness being so focused on the moment, what is going on inside of me, and the words I hear. Without question or pause, there is an urgent and immediate need for me to speak and make a connection between the living and the spirit world. That is the only way I can describe it. I am not the only one who has experienced this phenomenon. I am sure you have heard tennis players speaking of "playing in the zone" where they feel they reach their peak performance.

Pele, the great soccer player, wrote of his experience of being in the zone in his autobiography, <u>My Life and Beautiful Game</u>, "In the middle of a match, I felt a strange calmness I had not experienced before. It was a type of euphoria. I felt I could run all day without tiring, that I could dribble through any or all of their team, which I could almost pass through them physically. It was a strange feeling and one that I had not had before. Perhaps it was merely confidence, but I have felt confident many times without that strange feeling of invincibility."

Similar to the experience described by Pele, once I enter the "zone" I can, if necessary, stay in that state all day without tiring. Of course, my life does not allow for such a luxury given car pooling and doing homework with the boys! The feeling is of almost a tangible wall of calm, which again blocks out all around me except for the person for whom the message is focused.

Accordingly, "living in the moment" takes on a whole new meaning. The moment before me is all that seems to exist. My thoughts go nowhere except to the present — the here and now. There are no thoughts of my own racing through my head; my thoughts are all pushed aside for me to "hear," "see" and "feel" what is coming through to me from the spirit world. I just funnel information from my senses. Sometimes I listen and then speak, most times I just know. My mouth opens and out come the words. Out come descriptions that I do not actually see but just know. Other times, I feel in my very core and every cell of my body what I then go on to describe. I might "feel" someone wearing a blue sweater. How can that be since typically colors aren't felt? All I can say is that in my world they are. The experience almost defies description.

I also feel this way when I meditate and connect. Once again I enter a space where time is suspended. It is like being in a vacuum or a black hole. Sometimes the feeling will pass; other times I must rally myself up and out. I always pray and ask for protection before I meditate which allows me to enter a safe space where protection abounds. I become a breathing entity; I just am; an open vessel through which the energy of the universe flows through me.

Mark Richardson, a British athlete, said of being in the zone: "It is a very strange feeling. It is as if time slows down and you see everything so clearly. You just know that everything about your technique is spot on. It just feels so effortless; it is almost as if you are floating across the track. Every muscle, every fiber, every sinew is working in complete harmony and the end product is that you run fantastically well." — Extracted from Mind Games, Grout and Perrin, 2006.

While I am in this zone, I feel as though my energy is one with the energy of the universe. As though my body is reduced to those little white specks we see when a light shines through the darkness - just floating. If the "living" person to whom I am speaking tries to provide me with information by way of explanation (usually because they are excited and stunned) it disrupts my focus and I must tell them not to speak. It is important for people to just answer "yes" or "no." There is no doubt as to what I must say and like a dart to a target, say it I will. Sometimes, I am sorry to say, I can sound rude in telling people not to talk, but it is necessary for me to receive and not feel as though I am being fed information. I sense the information in a uniquely strange way filling me and prompting me to speak, even when I least expect it. This happens frequently with my group of friends. Thank the Lord that they are accustomed to me by now!

Usually, when I begin, they recognize the signs, and I hear in the background someone blurt, "Here she goes again!"

And so it goes in suburbia; women get to together with other women as support groups or just to talk to others who understand their busy lives. A group of close friends and I formed a spiritual group that initially met every other week. We would sit around and talk (not like Bunco – no wine and prizes to win!) and explore each other's spirituality to help and heal each other, ourselves, and our families. One morning the women were talking (about what, to this day I could not tell you) and I felt myself begin to drift out. Now mind you, I allow it. If I am not in a place that I feel comfortable, or if the time was inappropriate I can stop it. It is not as if I am being possessed or taken over; that is not what I feel. Besides, given my predilection to be a bit of a "control freak", a trance would not bode well for me at all! Instead, again, it is a focus issue. That warm calm wall began to slowly build around me and blanket my senses. I became very conscious of each beat of my heart. My muscles seemed to relax and my mind emptied. Turning my head and, bolding interrupting their conversation without even a "pardon me", I blurted out to the two friends on my right side, "there is a man standing between the two of you."

Now, you may ask if I actually saw him. Not as I see a physical person, but close to that. At first, I just knew he was there and that he had blond hair and wore a blue v-neck sweater, shorts and tennis shoes. I also knew he was a terrible tennis player! When one of the women claimed him as a friend whom she knew in college, the visions and the words began to flow quickly. Again, once the connection is validated the spirit world takes that as a "green light." And, as often happens, when one spirit connects, other spirits see this as their way in as well. My friend's grandparents showed up and passed on very specific information that only she or her family could validate.

At one point, my friend began to interject some information and I rudely told her to stop. Given that these women love me, and know me, they just accepted it. Of course, I apologized and explained to her afterward that I am not meaning to be rude, but do not want the reading ruined by my own insecurities. If information is told to me by the living, I question what I hear, see and know. I feel a responsibility to keep the reading pure and unadulterated from anything anyone in the room has to say.

By the end of my rambling, my friend did not know what had hit her. As she was overcome with emotion, and as tears streaked down her cheeks, she reminded me of a conversation we had a few weeks prior. At that time she had complained that I had not yet read her. Well, be careful what you ask for! She was so shaken by the information, that to this day, we have had many conversations, but never have we spoken about that incident. The information was for her to process and to induce her to heal in some way. I am just the messenger and often do not know what transpires in someone's heart and mind after the session. Additionally, usually I do not remember the specifics of what I say. I remember in general and I remember some things that may stick out in my mind, but if I speak for an hour, I recall maybe five minutes. The message is not for me. Frequently, I do not always understand the information that is being passed on. However, at times, I do understand more than other times, because I am told to clarify. It is all very strange, even if you ask me. But as strange as it is, this experience helps people to heal their wounds.

Okay, so now that I went through all of that, you may ask, is it always that way? NO! Other times, I do not enter a zone but there is simply an all knowing feeling as the words just pop out of my mouth. On the other hand, if I know that I will be conducting a reading, prior to the appointed time, I meditate and take notes on what the spirits and my spirit guides tell me. These notes give me a head start on my sessions with their loved ones here on earth. It also helps me to connect and "meet" the spirits with whom I will be working and for whom I will be speaking. It is comforting for me and for them. Once the connection is made, they can easily get my attention and send me information while I am doing the reading.

Now, there is one more thing: the way in which the experience happens is fluid and ever changing! Maybe next week it will happen in a different way, who knows. As the receiver, I am open to the way that may be best for all concerned. You know, like the new math, there is never just "one way!"

~Nine~

Coffee, Muffins and the Dead!

*If God had wanted me otherwise, He would
have created me otherwise.*
Johann von Goethe

After years of hearing, seeing and talking to spirits, the
day came when I knew it could not be something that I
should be coveting with my friends and family any longer.
When a good friend of mine, Michelle, suggested that I read
a group of her friends, with whom I had never been
acquainted, I felt compelled to say yes. I felt obliged because
Michelle was not going to take no for an answer! This was a
bit unnerving for me. I know that my friends love me and in
their love I feel comfort and respect. I can be who I am and
do what I do without wondering about whether or not I am
being judged. But with strangers? Could I actually do it? I
recognized that I was being tested. If I put my faith in God,
my entire trust, it would work out. Yet, my ego was
screaming, "what if I fail?" I wondered if these women, all
from my town, would see me in the local supermarket, Stop
& Shop, and point me out as the lunatic who thought she
could talk to the spirit world! In the end, my trust in the
universal forces won out and into God's hands I placed

myself — ego and all. And so, for once and for all with all the courage I could muster, out among strangers I ventured and permitted my gift to flow and my mission to be recognized. I would stand erect and be the messenger from heaven in the middle of suburban Connecticut. So after over forty years of having conversations that I only shared with a select few, my world began to expand and grow.

The day I was to do my first "public reading" at Michelle's gracious home was a hectic one. My whole family was helping my younger son with a project the previous night. That morning my older son, who had a serious case of high school "senioritis" was preparing for AP exams and a prom that he was going to on Saturday. It was close to the end of the school year and the pace was picking up. So once again, there I was on a tight rope trying to balance my family in both arms! As I sat on the living room sofa, arranging the pillows around me for comfort and preparing to meditate for the upcoming group reading, I thought, "What have I gotten myself into?" I questioned whether or not the timing was right. But, when I give my word, I stick to it, so there was no turning back. Finally, after a time, as my mind and body quieted, on the pad set before me, I wrote whatever came to my mind. When I felt the energy of the spirit world depart and looked down at the pages of writing before me, I knew I was armed and ready to go.

On the way to Michelle's house, out of nowhere it hit me that my son did not call the florist to order a corsage for his prom date. Matthew showing up with no corsage would have been a monumental crisis. The teenage drama would have been cataclysmic. I could hear his voice in my head, "No corsage? Oh my God, what will she think of me? Everyone will think that I am a loser! Will I ever get a date again?" So, being the good mom that I am (and because I could not bear to go through the trauma of Matthew not having the corsage), after parking my car, I literally ran into Michelle's house. As the women who were gathered for the reading watched, like a mad woman, I rushed passed them into the kitchen and scrambled for the phone numbers of florists in the area. After a few phone calls, I was able to locate a florist who was still taking orders – the prom is a big thing in any town, and most boys, or their moms, order the corsages well in advance!

As is par for the course of my life, the florist, upon hearing my voice over the phone line, without ever having met me, took the giant leap from the topic of flowers to telling me, in great detail, about all of his physical problems. This happens to me all the time – no matter where I am. They say when the student is ready the teacher appears. Likewise, when the person is ready to heal, the healing facilitator appears. So, as the conversation on the phone dragged on for a few minutes, a very patient group of women were waiting for me in the other room. When I finally got off the phone, Michelle quickly ushered me into her little library and commanded me to "meditate!" And so I tried to relax and meditate. Nothing happened. As I felt a tinge of anxiety, I implored my guides, "You cannot leave me hanging here. Help me." At that moment I felt a calm energy literally blanket me from the top of my crown to my toes. I was not in my zone, but I was basking in serenity.

Soon the women gathered in the library with me. I felt their nervousness and curiosity. Michelle had told them that I had never had an "arranged" reading with a group of strangers. They did not know what was going to happen, if anything at all. As they took their places in the circle, I thought "Here I go", and right then and there, I began to soar. Informing them of the protocol I like to follow and exactly what was going to transpire in the next hour or two, I spoke for a few minutes to set the energy in the room and to merge and feel comfortable with their energy. Years of energy work had prepared me to recognize that establishing an energy continuum was important in order for the spirits to ease through. I explained to these very curious women that I was a messenger for the spirit world, not a fortune teller or a magician. I explained that death does not kill or destroy love; love never dies. It goes on forever. And this love makes it possible for those on the other side of the veil to touch us over and over again through their presence and their words.

And with those words of love leaving my lips, the reading began. I started the session by conveying the words and messages that I had written on my pad while meditating that morning. It was miraculous! The first message was a description of an intricate design on a turquoise necklace, which a female spirit was showing me. As I described the necklace and the spirit in detail, at once one of the women broke in and excitedly told the group of the significance of this necklace and her relationship to the spirit presenting it. Once she started speaking the spirit on the other side began to pour specific information like water from a spigot. At that moment, I felt a rush of energy and knew that I was doing what I had been born to do. Without thinking, in the middle of this group of amazed women, in utter and profound joy, I threw my hands up in the air and yelled, "I can do it!"

After relaxing and tucking my feet under my butt, I continue to read these wonderful women for two more hours. They cried, they laughed but more importantly they healed as they were once again united with those they loved. The energy frequency in the room elevated and even those, who never recognized shifts in energy, felt the presence and energy of the spirits who were with us that day.

People are always asking if our pets go on to the other side and visit us here on the earth plain. Well, at this reading a much-loved pet did come through. I saw a big dog sitting by the side of a very poised and quiet woman who sat directly in front of me. It was clear that he was protecting her and would not leave her side. He kept telling me he loved her and would always be with her. Yes, telling me! I also heard, in English, a Hungarian spirit, who in life did not speak a word of English. Now, think about this, if the dog and a human spirit want to communicate with their loved one through me, barking, howling or speaking a language that I cannot translate would be a total waste of energy. I might think it was funny, but that is only because I have a strange sense of humor! Anyway, I hear each and every spirit that comes through to me in English. Sometimes it is not their words, but the feeling that I can translate into words. Sometimes I just know what they are saying without actually hearing the words. If they want to get their message through they will use whatever means works for them and me.

After a while, at this particular reading, it became apparent that all the spirits that were coming through were communicating within a "theme." Each one of them, although radically different personalities, from the boisterous Brooklyn Italian male to the demure, dapper Fred Astaire type, spoke about "legacy." They wanted to let their families know what they wanted, recognized or passed on. One spirit spoke at length and in great detail about the family china and specifically to whom she wished it given; another spoke of certain familial traits that he wanted recognized by those still living, and one spirit came through speaking about his Native American ancestry. The woman to whom this was directed, Joanne, who has blond hair and light skin, laughed and said that her grandfather always insisted that he was Native American but no one had ever validated his claim. Well, this spirit, her grandfather, kept insisting that he truly carried Native American blood and pointed out the necessity for Joanne to find her place in this ancestry and connect to the gene pool which was a part of her heritage. He was adamant that she and her daughters must reconnect to this part of the family lineage and carry it forward into future generations. Joanne just laughed remembering her grandfather's passion for storytelling, and said that she would try to find out as much as she could from her parents.

When Joanne went home that afternoon she called her parents to verify some of the information she had taken away with her — some of which was specifically about them. She laughed as she told her father that her grandfather, even from the other side, was insisting that he was a Native American. She was stunned when her father told her that his grandmother, his father's mother was indeed a Native American. Joanne could not believe that after years of thinking of her grandfather's stories as just creative imagination that his stories were true! She pondered the meaning of her grandfather coming through with instructions for her to reconnect to the Native American part of her heritage. A few days later, when she questioned me, my guides rang out loud and clear that she should research and recognize this woman, her great-grandmother. They told me that her great-grandmother's Native American Indian heritage was not spoken about since her marriage to Joanne's great-grandfather. My guides explained that given the prejudice of the era, his family frowned upon her ethnicity. And, so her lineage was buried with her.

Also, rather interestingly, Joanne's grandfather related during the reading that his Native American mother's family was involved in a very special practice. Although it was shown to me, it was not clear. It was up to Joanne to figure it out, learn and to carry it forward in her family. She had to invest the time and assume the responsibility for bringing the ancient traditions through for future generations.

I left Michelle's house that day feeling alive. And, the amazing exuberance of the day ran through the entire weekend. It was weeks later that I truly felt the impact of the day. I received a call from Maria, who was one of the group members, to thank me for changing a piece of her life. As previously mentioned, since I usually do not remember what the spirits say through me, she had to explain. Maria said that her relatives had given her a message about her son, which had put her at ease. She explained she had gone into the reading with her worries of her son weighing heavily on her. Through the communication with those on the other side and their specific messages in relation to her son, she was able to put her fears aside and relate to her son in a different way. Maria went on to say that she was happier and more at ease than she had been in many months. To me that is the bottom line. It is all about healing. That is the reason I put myself out there. That is my mission and my path in this life. It is all about the love that the spirits bring through to heal those still here. It is all about love.

~Ten~

So You Want? But What Do You Need?

If things are not as you wish, wish them as they are.
Yiddish Proverb

Many people, with whom I connect, want and desire certain gifts. They will read every book and try every class to learn and explore how to achieve this goal. They are attuned to every energy modality that comes their way. The search for more knowledge is wonderful; but sometimes that which we seek is not always that which we truly need or even what was intended for us. Sometimes, we overlook the most precious gifts which are standing right there in front of us. Yet, during a period of seeking, when we have opened our eyes (or so we think) the universe begins to thrust the unique gifts which we have always possessed in front of our faces. If we pay close attention, and recognize the workings of the universe and the particular gifts that we are to explore within ourselves, they unroll like a beautiful carpet in front of our eyes at every interval. If the person's eyes are open, they will realize what is going on and, hopefully, embrace the gifts. It is from one gift that another and another spring forth. On the other hand, if the person is adamant about the gifts they decide they want, they may push away their God given gifts unceremoniously and without gratitude. This is unfortunate.

As Americans we are taught to strive for that which *we decide we want*. We are taught there is no opposition that cannot be overcome and that there is an opportunity for everything. The United States is a wonderful country where everyone can achieve their goals. That is the reality of the physical plane. In this country, you are permitted a free public education, can go on to higher education, maybe take finance and math classes and become a banker, or an international financier. If that is your dream, so be it and go for it! You may pursue your dream of being an educator and teach high school English at a prep school, if that is what you desire. That is the way things progress in the school of the earth. Not so in the school of the universe.

The Spirit, the Divine, has bestowed certain gifts upon each of us. Each gift develops in the way that is best for us, and society at large. Yet, we cannot force the gifts that we want, when we want them. Rather, we can only open our minds and our souls to the broader view and be grateful for the wonderful gifts set before us. What a feast! There are so many plates that we can eat from and so many drinks to imbibe. Be grateful! I know it is difficult when you feel that you have not been graced as you see fit. But be grateful and acknowledge and USE the gifts that you have been given already and you just may attain your dream gift.

It comes down to patience as well. The heavens must get a real chuckle when I even think in that direction! I have never been known as one of the most patient of people dropped on this planet. Like many others, patience is a virtue that I have been seeking my whole life. Patience is the realization that we cannot control the unknown, that at some level we must accept who and what we are and that some things take more time for us to attain than for others. It is a challenge. I have said to God on numerous occasions, "If I can just do this or that, I can help so many more people. So why, why won't you let it be?" At times I receive answers; some answers I like and some I could do without; but the bottom line is that the answers are given. Maybe what I desired just was not meant to be at that moment in time. Maybe, just maybe, my journey had to be a bit different than I initially envisioned. Perhaps, our biggest lesson is surrender and trust. Give it up to the big Power in the sky! It is tough, I know; but I also know that it is necessary to do so for growth in the spiritual realm.

Years ago when I decided that I wanted to dive right into the healing arena, a good friend and teacher said to me, "You are a healer. Every time you open your mouth, people listen and they are healed. You do not even recognize your own abilities! Open your eyes and be who you were meant to be." Did I listen? Of course not! I took classes upon classes and learned techniques that I thought that I should know in order to fulfill my desire to heal in a certain way. Funny, in retrospect, in the end, I came full circle right back to where I started. My friend was right. The way in which I can help people is by talking and connecting with them, whether through the spirit world or my own intuition and insight. Yet, in the past, I persistently sought another means of fulfilling my mission and overlooked the gifts that I already possessed; the ones that were there at birth. In my stubbornness, I could not give up my quest to the universe; control was an issue. When I finally came to the end of my rope and said, "I accept", my world and my gifts flourished.

In hindsight, I am glad that I learned all the things that I have along the way, it was my own personal journey and it gave me the courage to ultimately do what I was meant to do with my life. It provided backbone and an understanding about what was going on with me, and those for whom I offer healing. My spiritual education provided me the wherewithal and confidence to do what I do regardless of outside perception of how crazy or funky. My gifts are precious to me — given to me to use, and so I do. It is part of the party that is my life; in appreciation it is to be used and enjoyed. So be it!

All that being said, my students are constantly asking me how to channel spirits. My answer is always the same. Move out of the fear and ego and into the light of courage and oneness with the universe. Have faith and then have more faith that if it be God's will, it will happen. We all possess a certain level of intuition; it is just a matter of opening up and letting the universe take control a bit. Each person will be able to move into their own space and use their own gifts through faith and gratitude. You may never be able to read people the way in which I do, but maybe you will feel problems in their auras, or see into their past and help heal in that way. Maybe you will feel drawn to teach and heal through your words, or just be there for the people in your life. Whatever it is, be aware of what keeps coming your way, and what you may be dismissing. Again, your gifts are probably right in front of your face! But you must have faith that there is someone or something out there in the great unknown that is watching out for you and will lead you to the feast.

Likewise, my gifts are very different than others who heal in similar ways. I do not channel spirits or go into a trance. Maybe that just does not sit right with my soul. I do not know and do not give it much thought. I am happy where I am and if more comes my way, it is all good. If no other gifts are left for me to open, that is good too. As a child of the universe, my faith is in hands that are larger and stronger than my own. It is really nice to be held and taken care of by the All Knowing Presence.

Thus, faith is not a word that is solely attached to "religion" per se. More importantly, it is necessary for the acceptance of our gifts and our journeys. When it comes to seeing, touching and becoming one with your spiritual gifts, you have to have faith. These are not gifts that you purchase at the supermarket or department stores; these gifts are elusive, intangible and are those which money cannot buy. They must be earned by believing. It is the belief in something greater than us; more powerful and with the means to lead us into the Divine Oneness and, thus, bestow Grace upon us. It is in believing in that which we cannot see; that which science cannot define. This is a difficult task for many. It is leaving our rational mind at bay and, again, putting our belief in that which we do not see; at least not in the conventional way. Faith flows through our veins as it has through the centuries for our ancestors. Every religion embraces a component of faith. It is in this faith; this knowing that there is even something greater than you, that you can ultimately magnify your soul and come into your own.

Many of us have had encounters that defy our intelligence and yet, we know they are authentic. The overwhelming ardor of the moment resonates in our souls. This tremendous feeling, whether it is love, awe or power, is so great that it unnerves us and although wonderful, is confusing to our limited perceptions of our universe. Yet, in the absence of any physicality, we know, without reservation that we are not alone. But what or who is out there? How does it change us? It is beyond anything we are taught in grade school. Yet, in this realization, we are changed. I, for one, would like to share the awe, humility and hope that I have taken away from these experiences and, hence, my quest to spread the word about the spirit world through this book. We are small and insignificant in light of the magnitude of the universe but we must be special or why would we have the ability to question and to be led to the answers? When we finally reach that moment of awareness, when we know beyond a shadow of a doubt, beyond all reasoning and intellectual understanding that we are so special that we are never left alone; we are humbled. It is in that moment our gifts begin to surface and to bloom that an awakening springs from our souls. It is awesome.

Faith is one of those words that by its very nature is elusive and begs us to ask and ponder its meaning. What is faith? And how does it fit into our lives? I once read that faith is the chair that supports us. We do not question why or how the chair can support our weight yet, when we sit, we know it will hold us.

Faith is the word that captures the essence of our souls. It is the belief in the Divine on a level that defies our intellect and our understanding. In Islam it is called "Iman" and is an instinct of the soul which completely and unquestionably submits to Allah. It includes belief, profession, and the body's performance of deeds consistent with Allah's will. Similar to Islam, in Buddhism, faith is an important element of the teachings of the Buddha and refers to a sense of conviction. While this belief does not imply "blind faith", it nevertheless requires a degree of blind faith. It centers primarily in spiritual attainment and belief in the Buddha as a supremely awakened being, as well as a belief in his superior role as teacher of both humans and gods and in the truth of his teachings. Faith in Buddhism propels the Buddhist practitioner towards the goal of awakening and nirvana. The goal of awakening implies the attainment of "sight", of knowing what we are all about.

Likewise, in the Judeo/Christian religions, faith is essentially a belief in that which is not physically manifested. Furthermore, in Judaism, faith is implicit in its doctrine of belief in a God that is unseen. Some of the most important acts of faith are found in the actions of Abraham who both accepts statements and directives from God that seem impossible, implausible and unconscionable. Yet, Abraham is obedient in his actions (Genesis 12:1).

Aware of the definition of faith as discussed above, Christianity takes faith to the highest level and is one of the most important topics in the teachings of Jesus Christ. Interpretations of faith in Christianity differ somewhat among various Christian traditions, yet basically faith is the hope for things which are not seen, but which are believed to be true (Heb. 11: 1). It is centered in Jesus Christ and his teachings.

Now, given all of this, there are those who accept their faith without question; without missing a beat. And then, there are those who question their faith at various points in their lives. In my youth, a Jesuit priest told me something that would stick with me forever. He said that true faith is born out of doubt and when we question and explore our beliefs, and recognize what we believe, we are brought to a deeper understanding of our beliefs. As I grew older, I realized the truth and depth of this statement.

Recently, I had a discussion with my priest. I have been struggling with certain aspects of my faith and beliefs. When I explained my problem, she told me that she was so excited for me. I looked at her thinking, "what is in that coffee cup?!?!" But, in her sobriety, she was serious.

"Excited? You must be kidding. It is so much easier to just accept." I retorted.

"Maybe," she expounded, "but you are coming to a deeper understanding of what you believe, which will lead you to a profound spirituality. Questioning is wonderful; it brings you to the answers."

Interesting. The potency of "questioning" is definitely a concept that is underused and underestimated. We should all explore what we believe and find the answers that make sense in our souls. If it is in the questioning, and the pondering that we are brought to the throne, to be open to more of our gifts, than I, for one, will ask away!

Given the elusiveness of faith, in believing that there is an Energy out there who hears us and can answer our pleas and give us the gifts we seek, what does it really come down to? What is it really about? What motivates those that are pure, and seek not to elevate themselves but act for the good of their souls and the souls of others? What motivates me? Sometimes the most profound answers come from little voices with innate wisdom. At those moments, we know we must listen.

Looking back at my own life, it certainly has been a progression. Through the years, my own gifts grew and grew. Sometimes I deviated from the path and moved into different directions, but all in all it was all growth towards the expansion of who I am and who I was meant to be. Do not get me wrong, I am not there yet. I have lots of growing to do. At times, my patience is tested, I want what I want and I want it now! Boy, when my kids have that attitude it makes me crazy! Can you imagine how God must feel? But it was all good and I had to learn to wait. I am still learning. I have faith that there is a plan, a map that my soul is following to lead me to my unique hidden treasures. In retrospect, in the past, if I did not hold onto my faith then I would have tried to control and just ran myself in circles. Of course, I did do a bit of that! It is so difficult to surrender and put our lives in someone else's hands; someone or something that we do not even see! So really what's it about? Always when I have these deep questions, one of my sons rises to the occasion and out of nowhere the answer is laid before me. This time it was Joseph who, once again, fulfilled the role of teacher.

For my birthday a couple of years ago, Vinny gave me a charm bracelet. It is a silver bracelet on which the charms slide on easily. Joseph, who was nine years old at the time, was examining all of the charms. He came to a charm inscribed in Japanese kanji and asked me for the translation in English.

"It means "love," I answered him.

He thought for a moment. "So love can look lots of different ways. It is not always spelled l-o-v-e. It can be different."

I looked at this little person who I helped create and thought if he really knew what he was saying to me; if he knew that he just spoke words that most adults were still attempting to understand.

Joseph had more to say; Joseph always has more to say! Rather matter-of-factly, he proclaimed, "I am going to buy you a charm that says "faith."

Similar to other mothers, I endeavor to protect my son from even a minor disappointment. In that frame of mind, I inquired, "That is wonderful Joseph, but how do you know that there will be charm that says faith?"

He looked at me with soulful deep chocolate brown eyes and answered patiently, as if he were speaking to a child. "Well," he began, "where there is love there is always faith."

In all Joseph's innocence, he summed up what the human race has been seeking to do for centuries. It is in our love and our desire to be loved and right with our God that we give up our intellectual understanding on some level and follow our souls and believe. It is in this faith that we are loved and our prayers are heard, and because of this desire to love and be loved that we seek to give the world more of ourselves. In this love, we strive to reach our highest potential and accept our gifts with courage and faith. Be patient, have faith and your love will shine through all that has been given to you.

~Eleven~

Who Were You?

Children who remember their past lives offer the most compelling evidence yet for reincarnation... when adults listen - really listen - to what the children are trying to say, their own understanding of spirit and of children are changed forever.
Carol Bowman, <u>Children's Past Lives</u>

Growing up Catholic, the topic of "past lives" did not come up. It was a taboo subject in our religion, so I just pushed the topic to a corner of my mind and left it there for many years. I was taught that people died and their souls went to heaven, or maybe not, that was it. There was no discussion about returning to live out karma, or fix unresolved problems or anything else. Death was the end of physical life. That is it — the end, no discussion. It was not a topic up for exploration, and truly no one really wanted to talk about it in my family. And so we didn't.

Yet, as I matured and my belief broadened, I sought clear, concise explanations on a variety of topics; one being reincarnation. I have read some compelling books on the possibility that there is some credence to returning again and again to this earth plane. Aside from my own spirit guide (who only recently made claim to having known me in a previous life), the spirits that I see, hear and feel for others, so far have not been interested enough to teach me and lead me to an answer to this question. They simply come through and use their energy to communicate with their loved ones. They are not really interested in me. So, here I do not have a real solid foundation for believing or not believing; just a gut belief and the words of my spirit guide.

It is reasonable to me that in order to actually be present with God, one's soul must be perfect and in accord with the Divine vibration. If life is a journey of healing, which I believe to be true, in which we are born to essentially heal ourselves and others, and thus, come closer to reaching perfection, what happens when perfection is not attained? Well, then it would be reasonable to believe that we have to fix what we did wrong. And it makes sense that we come back here to the earth and attempt to fix the wrongs. Since the "we" after death are "souls" without bodies, we are born to new families but experience the life issues or relationships that we need to fix — hence karma. If there is a relationship problem between two souls that needs repair, the two souls have to meet up again. That is why we are said to come back in soul clusters. We come back and hang out with the souls we have been with before – old friends, new bodies! So, maybe one of my sons was at one time my father and the other my mother! Heaven knows they think they are my parents in their all-knowingness! Maybe my husband was my son – make sense ladies?

Dr. Brian Weiss, a renowned psychiatrist, gives credence to reincarnation and has written the gospel on this subject in his books. Dr. Mehmet Oz, a noted cardiologist, and a tremendous voice for the field of alternative medicine and energy work, appeared with Dr. Weiss on Oprah, the TV talk show, and did not discredit his findings. By the way, Dr.

Weiss' books and theories have been around for a very long time. This is not new stuff, just stuff that is now coming to the forefront. We are in transition as a race and seem to be more willing to move to a different space in our consciousness and thus, our beliefs. There are studies upon studies, old and new, that are making many of us pause and think and perhaps even accept other viewpoints and beliefs.

Yet, as I mentioned, being a mother, much of my deep learning usually comes via one of my children. It was Joseph, who really made me think about the whole subject of past lives. And, Joseph, being Joseph, truly rocked my world through the story that follows. My perception of past lives has not and will never ever be the same.

It was a rainy day in the winter of 2000. As the wind and freezing pellets whipped against the window, I sat on my bed diligently writing out checks to pay our many bills. I was finding it difficult to give this task my entire focus given that Joseph, who was three at the time and not fully verbal (his premature birth resulted in a speech delay) was running in and out of my bedroom. Like most children, the minute the mother turns her thoughts and actions to something important, is speaking on the telephone or is in the bathroom, there is an urgent need for the child to demand her attention. At least that is how my children have always conducted themselves. When they were younger, the most important conversations were held while I was "relaxing" in the bathtub! Anyway, as my pen was poised in my hand, ready to write out the mortgage check, Joseph burst into my bedroom and insisted that I give him my undivided attention.

"Joseph," I calmly tried to reason with him (have you ever attempted to reason with a head strong three years old?) "Mommy is paying bills so that we can continue to live in this house. When I am done, I will play with you. Okay?"

"No. I want to play now!" Joseph screeched. And then he burst out, "I wish I was with my other mommy!"

Not having the patience that Mother Theresa possessed, I dismissed his words, hoping to finish my task. "Okay, so go find your other mommy." I said off-handedly, my eyes focused on the checks and bills spread across the bedspread in front of me.

"Well," Joseph proclaimed in his little voice filled with an undeniable maturity, "I would, but she's dead."

His words hit me like a ton of bricks. What did he say? I stopped writing and stared at him completely baffled yet unnerved by his confident words. What was he talking about? He did not know or even comprehend what dead meant. In his world, dead meant: 'Bang! Bang! You are dead!' And then you stand up and have apple pie. As calmly as I could muster, I asked him what he was talking about.

What came out of his mouth next, forever changed my way of thinking about past lives. The topic of past lives moved from one that I did not think about to one that I began to give much thought to and explore. It was after that conversation on that dismal, windy, rainy afternoon that I began to research, read about and question my own beliefs about reincarnation. It was my son, a three-year-old baby, who opened the gates in my mind and heart and set me on a new path.

"I am talking about my other family. I lived with my mommy and daddy in a big house with a white swing on a big porch. I had lots of brothers and sisters and we had to share our bed with each other. It was squashy but fun! They were nice. I miss them all."

He paused as if he were done. But I was not done. He had been given the opportunity to gaze into an open window that I did not know existed and, although I was a bit confused, I wanted to know more.

"What happened to you?" I implored.

Again, with his huge liquid brown eyes peering into my soul, he patiently explained. "I grew up. I got married and had two kids. Everyday I put on a white coat and went to work. And then I got really, really old and died."

I was stunned. What was my child saying to me? I wanted more. I needed more.

"Joseph, what happened after you died?"

"I went up to heaven. It was beautiful and I played with all the angels. I liked heaven." Joseph spoke so clearly (unlike his usual self) and the words poured from his mouth with the ease of a recent memory.

I thought for a moment and asked, "Joe baby, if heaven was so wonderful, why are you here now?"

And here my son, my baby, blew me out of the water. Joseph looked at me as though he were an old wise man. His gaze, like a lightening bolt, electrified my entire being as his beautiful brown orbs conveyed the pure, unconditional love he felt for me. Before he even spoke I was bowled over by the emotion that was radiating from him.

Joseph stared straight into my eyes and with all his heart he said very slowly and very simply, "Because you needed me."

As soon as the words flowed from his tiny pink lips, the tears began to stream down my face. In that minute our relationship was defined forever. It was one of those moments that I will remember for the rest of my life. As Rose Fitzgerald Kennedy once said, "Life is not a matter of milestones, but of moments." In that one moment, as this little soul stood before me and told me that he gave up heaven to be with me, to help me, because I needed him to, my perception of life was changed and I truly understood what love is all about. Joseph gave me the best gift that I will ever receive. As I held him to my own heart, he hugged me, wiped my tears and ran inside, and into the tomorrows that waited for him, only to forget our conversation. But I never will.

While I sat on my bed, now alone, Joseph's words hung like a quiet mist in the air. My face wet with tears, my heart filled with the love for my son, I felt as though I was in a dream and I did not know what to do. I knew I had to share this with someone. So I called my very Catholic mother and relayed the entire episode. I do not know what I expected her to say. In retrospect, it would have been more apt for her to discount the whole discussion as nonsense from the mouth of a babe. But she did not. After the entire incident was relayed, she was quiet. Then, in the commanding voice that only a mother can use and get away with, my mother who did not believe in reincarnation, told me to believe every word that Joseph said to me. And so, I did, and I do.

I cannot prove reincarnation; nor can I prove the story of my son's past life. The religion I grew up with does not support the belief; I do not even know if the church I attend now does. It does not matter. I do know, without a doubt, that what my baby said to me that day was from his heart and a place of all knowing. And, so without question or pause, I have to believe; I do believe. My belief is fuzzy at times, but I am open to learn more and explore the possibility. More than that, I would love to help others explore this topic. That day will come. But for the here and now I am a student of the universe and will learn as it is fit for me. Again, from the mouth of the innocent came a great lesson. Joseph opened a door, and I have opened the windows to let the breeze of knowing in.

~Twelve~

I Just Keep Getting in the Way!

Ego: The fallacy whereby a goose thinks he's a swan
Author Unknown

We all have the potential to carry out greatness. However, we are not greater than any other living thing on this planet. We have the power to bring compassion, healing and light. Yet, we are not the Power and we are only the bearers of light, not the light itself. There is a difference - a huge difference. Our egos have a problem with the difference and not being the "Power." As a result, our egos, in their quest for supremacy, attempt to separate us from Divinity, thus portending greatness, instead of embracing the Truth and the true Power. The ego pulls a woolen hat over our eyes so that we cannot see the Truth. Our egos defy the fact that we are small in the scheme of things and that although, we embrace and carry Divinity, we are not God. We are not greater or more powerful than anyone or anything else. We are cogs in the wheel of the universe that just help to keep it spinning. That does not mean we are insignificant; every cog is needed for the wheel to spin. Our lives are not to control and elevate ourselves, but rather to find peace on this planet and love – a peaceful cohesiveness.

Nevertheless, the ego is an essential ingredient in the batter, the make up, of who we are individually and collectively. It is that part of each of us which embodies pride, conceit, narcissism and self-infatuation. The ego advocates the need to be separate from everyone and everything else. The ego says "I am better, greater, and smarter." It is the demon that lives inside each of us that thrives on power and control. It will breathe fire on anyone and any thought that is good which may impede upon its territory in order to rein as superman. This fire breathing demon relishes in elevating us to something we are not. And in the extreme case, the ego believes it is God.

In the movie "The Silence of the Lambs", Hannibal Lecter, a psychotic serial killer, believed he had the right to take life and kill because he truly believed he was God. This is an extreme case of the irrational augmentation of the ego. The ego lives in fear of its own death; what would we each be, individually, without our own feelings of superiority or our individual ultimate greatness? That is a fear that we harbor in our egos. It is the fear of "oneness", which translates into "sameness." It is the fear of losing our uniqueness. Our egos strive to be at the top of the ladder, alone.

In relation to healing work, as well as, working with the spirit world, it is of utmost importance to stay aware of and to keep the ego at bay. Because of our society's lack of understanding in this area, they elevate the medium or healer to a pseudo-god. The belief is that mediums, spiritual healers, can give us the answers that we may not be able to attain ourselves, or so we think. Please, speaking as one of those "healers", do not make me into something or someone that I am not. Don't elevate me; I am just the messenger and the conduit. Truly, when my ego gets in the way, which it does at times, I am very conscious to open my eyes a bit wider and remember that it is not about me; I am just an open channel, but the gratitude goes to God. Even when I provide my energy and healing work in exchange for money or gifts, which goes to me, the universe and God are to be given all the gratitude and credit for endowing me with such gifts to be shared.

It is important that not only the people watching and experiencing a spiritual medium be conscious of who the "god" is, but the medium him or herself. I have seen people do this work and claim the full glory. They attribute their success to their own power and glory. Pooh! That is a lot of hooey! What power? What glory? I am elated when the words hit the right cord with someone and have the ability to heal. I feel the power of God, not my own power, careening through my veins. My head gets light and I am floating on a cloud. This happens every time. I recognize fully that I am so blessed to be able to partner with God in order to help others. That is it — pure and simple.

A while back, one of the great spiritual intuitives of our times was speaking at a local college. I had read all of her books but had never been in her presence or even heard her voice for that matter. Her books, to me, read smoothly and are very familiar. I came close to worshiping her for what she gave me as I rode the avenue of the printed word. And so, I went to see her in person. What a surprise! Her voice was anything but sweet and she lacked patience and tact with the audience! It was an eye opener. Her message was still profound but she was just the vessel; she was human and deeply flawed like the rest of us. I felt like I was hit with a bolt of lightening. She was a mortal, not God. Unfortunately, very few of us are as enlightened as Mother Theresa, who even experienced human weakness. If you saw me in the middle of a heated argument with Matthew, ranting and raving, totally out of control, you would know that I certainly am not the "Power." I am just me, a human being with lots of flaws.

I admit that my soul is elevated, as well as my vibration, when I am conducting healings and readings, but it is the Divine working within me, not me working within the Divine. You know the difference. So, be careful on whose head you place the crown; there is only one "King." Please don't make anyone's head big enough to think that the crown should be placed on their head. In time, the gold will begin to fade, the diamonds will fall out and it will prove to be too heavy. It will ultimately be their demise as the world sees the crown tumbling down.

~Thirteen~

Love is the Beginning and the End – It is the All

I believe that imagination is stronger than knowledge — myth is more potent than history — dreams are more powerful than facts — hope always triumphs over experience — laughter is the cure for grief — love is stronger than death.
Robert Fulghum

The strength and power of love is equal to none. There is nothing greater. It is the alpha and the omega. And, without question, it is the reason that those on the other side make contact to the living. But, sometimes we are floored by who comes through and maybe even a bit disappointed. We might be expecting our parents, siblings, grandparents and yet, the spirits that sometimes push their way in may be people we touched just for a moment in our lives. This experience teaches us that it is the moment that is defining. The impact of one small touch can equal a hundred hugs. It is all in the moment.

Also, spiritual healing takes many forms. It is not just the "laying on of hands", or the medical doctor with his bag of tricks, it goes far beyond the conventional means, both traditional and alternative. It is living a life of giving and helping others. It is found sometimes in the silence and the comfort of our prayers, or just a simple touch. Sometimes it is simply about showing compassion and love or just being there. As the modern day mystic Sai Baba said, "Love one another and help others to rise to the higher levels, simply by pouring out love. Love is infectious and the greatest healing energy."

There was a woman who attended one of my early group readings who longed to speak with a family member who had passed on. This was not to be. The spirits that came through spoke of their devotion to her based upon what she did for them in their last moments of life. They were not her relatives, yet they came through with an intensity and purity of emotion that was overwhelming to everyone in the room.

On that particular day, I had been reading a group of six women for about two and a half hours. Even though I was full of energy, my throat was getting sore. Yet, there was one woman in the room that had not been fortunate enough to have anyone from the other side make contact with her. She was so quiet and seemed to hang on every word that left my mouth; even though the words were not for her. As it sometimes happens during a reading, people may doze when the information is being funneled towards the others. But this woman had stayed focused and alert, absorbing the entire experience. She seemed to be in a rapture just listening, even though nothing and no one was present and speaking with her.

Finally, when I turned my attention to her, I saw the fluttering of angels all around her body. I looked down at the pad that held the dictation I had taken from my guides. I asked her if her name was Melissa to which she said it was.

Melissa's energy began to shimmer; a golden haze encompassed her entire body. As I gazed at her and began to speak, her eyes began to fill will soft tears that ran down her face unashamedly. Melissa did not wipe them away; she just let them flow.

As I observed her, the serenity and goodness of her persona emanated and shined from within her core. I heard her guides tell me of her kindness and her devotion to Mary, the Mother. Then I heard a chorus of spirits singing their love and appreciation for this wonderful woman. What I felt and saw was nothing short of amazing.

"Melissa, there are many spirits trying to communicate with you today. They are all thanking you for helping them. Some of them are telling me that they heard you when you spoke to them when they were in comas. I am hearing them say that although you thought they could not hear you, they did hear you."

I started to feel disoriented and confused and asked, "Melissa, do you work with people who have Alzheimer's or dementia?"

As her tears continue to flow unashamedly, Melissa softly answered, "Yes, I work in a nursing home."

"Okay, the ones that had Alzheimer's are saying that they spoke with you telepathically. They understood what you were saying to them. They appreciate your patience. They are thanking you. But there are others, who are saying that you were the last one with whom they spoke before moving onto the other side. They are thanking you for holding their hands and talking to them and giving them comfort. They are saying they had no relatives present and you helped them cross over. You told them to cross over. They are singing and telling me that they are praying for you

111

constantly and that when you cross over they all will be waiting to bring you to their open arms."

I conveyed all of this rapidly so that I would not lose the beautiful images these spirits were presenting to me. I saw the bright light surrounding big, wide-open arms that would greet Melissa someday.

Yet, I thought their description of death without relatives or friends, even in a nursing home was peculiar, and so I inquired, "Melissa why weren't their relatives present when these souls passed on?"

Melissa's face lit into a smile as she explained, "I work in a nursing home for Catholic nuns. They are very old and most of them do not have relatives present at the time of death so I stay with them."

Now it was clear to me.

"Melissa, they are telling me that you are a great healer. What do you do?"

"I am a nurse."

"You are not a great healer because you are a nurse, but because you love these people so much that your love has helped them progress to the other side. You are instrumental in helping them move on."

At this point, Melissa, as well as others in the room, were streaming tears from their eyes. She was now dabbing her eyes repeatedly with the crumpled tissue in her hand.

Even as I write about her, the heat in my hands is mounting; a signal to me of the healing power. This woman held so much healing energy in her hands and her body and, more importantly, in her heart. She gave so much to the women with whom she worked. Because she worked with women on the brink of death, she did not form relationships with them when they moved about their lives; she simply and profoundly was the catalyst to help them move on to the other side. The brief time she spent with these dying nuns, this moment in time, signified a big part of her purpose in this life and defined the death of each of these women. They loved her although they only knew her as the living angel that helped them move to their heaven. And from that vantage point, they prayed and guarded her, and someday will help her move on as well.

Amen.

~Fourteen~

I Want to Speak with My Mother!

Sincerity is the way of heaven.
Confucius, The Wisdom of Confucius

I promised my guides and myself that if I were to bring messages from the other side; I would convey only what they presented to me. I rely upon my guides to help me translate at times, but never do I "make-up" what is being relayed to me. I know there are a lot of charlatans out there who give people what they want to hear either to make more money, or just to appear to be the "real thing." In the end, the mask will fall. This is not what I do.

The spirit world devotes an enormous amount of energy to communicate, how dare anyone mangle the message. Moreover, hearing a message no matter who it is from on the other side should be riveting and wonderful to everyone on the earth. Yet, so many people are disappointed that they did not hear from the one with whom they wanted to connect. They become annoyed and frustrated when the message is not what they had hoped to hear or from whom they had wanted to connect. Being the messenger, I will only be the "messenger." In other words, my job is to bring the essence of the spirit to the person whether through the emotions,

114

personality or the words that I hear. That is it. I am conscious of separating "me" out of the equation. This does not always make everyone happy, but I have to be true to who I am and what I am doing.

As I said, sometimes it is difficult to make people understand that if they want to communicate with the other side as purely and unimposing as possible, they must keep information to themselves. When I ask a question, a simple yes or no will suffice. Yet, people get so excited that they want to tell me the "whole story." While I understand this and am so happy for their exuberance, it just makes my job that much more complicated. I do not want to be fed information. My job is not to regurgitate what the living is broadcasting to me. I would rather remain a blank slate, a chasm of emptiness, and just observe, listen and sense as the other side fills in the gaps. Again, my goal is to speak what the other side intends and desires to convey, not what I want to say or what anyone may want to hear. Sometimes they are one in the same; yet other times the desires of the living are at odds with those of the spirit world.

Early on, when I first started to give group readings, Andrea came to the first two sessions held. During the first session nothing came through for her, and she had to leave early for a previously scheduled appointment. While planning the second group reading, the hostess told me that Andrea really wanted to connect with her grandfather. Andrea had hoped that he would come through even though he professed a disbelief in the afterlife during his time on this planet. The hostess, meaning well, went on to give me bits and pieces of information about Andrea's grandfather and other members of her family.

On the morning of the next session, Andrea, as well as a group of women I had never met, entered the room in which I was to be giving the reading. The reading went on for two hours or so of wonderful information for everyone in the group, and two other women who just happened to stop by. Nothing came through for Andrea.

The hostess, being the kind person she is, suggested that I focus on Andrea to see if I could obtain any information at all from her relatives who had passed on. After attempting a couple of different ways, it was apparent that I could not connect. My mind just kept going back to the knowledge that was previously passed along to me about Andrea and her family. Either she wasn't ready to hear and understand, or, maybe, the problem resided with me. The bottom line was that nothing and no one was coming through.

"Andrea," I said, "I think I know too much information about your relatives. I am so afraid that what I am seeing and hearing is a figment of my imagination and I won't go there. Unless I believe the information to be pure and not from me, it is impossible for me to connect."

Andrea looked at me sadly and obviously very disappointed. My guides at that moment asked me to ask her if she believed in the spirit world.

"Well I don't know . . . I am an atheist." Andrea proclaimed.

"So, why are you here?" I innocently asked.

I was not intending to be glib, just curious. I always ask when people tell me of their disbelief while attending one of my readings. It fascinates me how the spirit world brings enlightenment to people.

"Well, I believe that there is a Power or something greater than us, I just do not call it God."

I heard my guides chuckle and begin to prompt me to speak.

"Andrea, believing that there is a Power greater than us out there somewhere, whether or not you call it God, or Bob or just "Some Power", is contrary to atheism. You may not subscribe to any one religion but that does not define what you believe. A common definition of an atheist is someone who does not believe in God. So we are compelled to ask, what or who is God? A power? A spirit? A person? The energy of the universe? That is up to you to decide, and thus, defines your own spirituality."

She looked at me a bit sheepishly, shrugged and smiled.

"Maybe 'atheist' is the wrong word." She said as my guides and her guides were busy chatting away.

"Our guides are telling me that before you connect to the other side, you must educate yourself. Start to read some books on spirituality. Andrea, they are saying you need to find your place. The focus, for now, is you. It is not about those on the other side. You have to take responsibility and help yourself. When the time is perfect for you, they will come through loud and clear."

I recommended some books to her that our guides indicated she should read. She was obviously very cerebral and needed to analyze and make sense of her world and her own spirituality.

However, this did not alleviate the disappointment. She still wanted to hear from the other side about more specific and verifiable things. I could not help her because they wanted her to first help herself get on track. I do not know why; it is not up to me to make that judgment. I wanted to make her happy and help her connect with her grandfather. I just could not. The message was the message.

Yet, the hostess questioned whether my guides were passing on the information or whether it was just my opinion. This startled me a bit since I had just spent two and a half hours relaying specific, and verifiable information; all of which, it was very apparent, I had no prior knowledge. But, I guess it was a fair question given that Andrea was clearly disappointed.

I answered in the best way I knew how.

"If a spirit or spirit guide is communicating through me, I pass on what they are saying to me. Unless I indicate that it is my opinion, my opinions and advice never come into play. I will say when the spirit surfaces, which is only fair since the only voice you hear is mine. How else would anyone be able to differentiate? Likewise, I will also say when I am speaking my own opinion."

Again, although my explanation was accepted and Andrea went on to purchase the recommended books, and was exposed to new and different views of spirituality, she was still very disappointed. The responsibility for her was to overcome the disappointment and take this wonderful message and allow it to grow and resonate in her soul. No one, but Andrea, could do this for her. It was absolutely her sole responsibility. We cannot manipulate those on the other side or get them to say what we think we need to hear. They know better. They are in a position to see and know all. We are at their mercy when it comes to communication.

Also, as the story related above indicates, never give any information to the medium with which they can use. Allow the spirits to do the work! And always, be thankful for each and every little bit of heavenly advice. You have free will, do with it what you will, but always be thankful for anything coming through the spirit realm. It takes a lot of love and energy to get their messages across to us.

Once more, it is also very important to move out of the way of your ego or what you think is best for you. Have an open mind. Sometimes Spirit or the spirits on the other side will give advice, not predict the future, but just give advice. Sometimes people do not want to hear the truth or what is contrary to what they believe about themselves. Frequently, when these messages come through it would be wise to take heed by just giving thought and consideration to the message. In the end, its your life to lead the way you see fit.

For instance, on another occasion a relative came through to a woman for whom I was doing a reading and told her to pay more attention to her younger daughter. This spirit conveyed that the other children demanded much of her time and the younger child was floundering in the absence of attention. Well, my client became enraged. This was not true, she told me. How could I say these things when I did not even know her or her children? She ranted and raved, which I patiently permitted. I am only the messenger. Six months later, she called me. She said that after thinking about the reading for a good month, she decided to make an effort to give her child more attention. As a result her daughter began to bloom before her eyes. The little girl was happier and more alive. Even her other children seemed happier. Point in fact, those on the other side know more than we do. Of course, if something sounds so wrong, it may be; but having an open mind may allow you to see your life and the lives of your family members through different colored glasses.

~Fifteen~

No Crystal Ball Here

You are led through your lifetime by the inner learning creature, the playful spiritual being that is your real self. Don't turn away from possible futures before you're certain you don't have anything to learn from them. You're always free to change your mind and choose a different future . . .
Richard Bach

There are those that are gifted with insight into the darker realm in order to help society. These people help the FBI and other law enforcement agencies find abducted children as well as criminals. They also help in finding the sites of homicides and the victims of violent crimes. They see, feel and relive horrific experiences in order to allow justice to prevail and help society. We should applaud these people who so willingly enter the darker side of this world and utilize their gifts to help us. I am sorry to say that my lack of courage and deep empathy and sensitivity prevent me from doing that type of work. I know that it would destroy me. From the beginning I refused to see into the darker realm. I am a bit of a wimp and coward. I am comfortable with the happier side of the spirit world. I want to pass on the love from the other side and visa versa. I do not see decaying bodies, blood or anything even close to a horror movie scene. Do not get me wrong; sometimes there is pain, either emotional or physical, but nothing like that being shown to these psychic detectives. It is not my niche, not my comfort zone. I leave that work for others who are so much more equipped than I.

Also, I am not a "fortune teller." Although I receive premonitions at times, I am very leery about predicting events. I may pass on that I have a "feeling" of something, but that is usually as far as I will go. I certainly cannot predict anything for my family. My husband has learned to be attuned to and not deny my hunches, or my intuition, but even these foresights are not clearly defined. When my son was applying to colleges, he was so very frustrated that I could not tell him which colleges would accept him. I could only relate where I thought he would not go. It is very difficult, as it is for most mediums, to read for their families. As a medium and a mother and wife, I am far too invested emotionally with my family to be an objective observer of the spirits and their messages.

On that note, many people seek out spiritual mediums, or psychics to read their future in lieu of for their own healing. Life can be difficult, and understandably, people want answers and reassurance that all their problems will pass and that the future will be brighter than the present. Some people go to mediums as a pseudo-therapy or as a crutch to help them with their broken dreams. They want to be told what will happen and thus prepare for the event. Of course, in preparing for the event, they can make the foretold event a reality.

Furthermore, keep in mind that a foretold event can be blocked as well. If the person hearing of the event, decides to fight it; in all reality it will not happen. Take the person who is told that he will be promoted at his job in the next month. Upon hearing the news, he decides that he does not want to work at that firm so he quits. Well, what of the prediction? We carry the responsibility for our lives and our path. It is contrary to our existence to push that responsibility to another person. By putting our trust in a psychic or a fortuneteller undermines the responsibility, the cause and effect and that which we create as we live each day. We are responsible for our future; we create it. If we are aware; we can see where we are going.

Accordingly, predicting the future is tricky business. As beings who possess free will, we can create and recreate our paths, our journeys at any moment in time. Anyone can plant a seed in someone's mind that the person may be able to orchestrate and make into his or her reality. The prediction of the future is more of a suggestion of what might happen if a certain path is chosen. How can anyone know the inner workings of someone's soul? I, for one, do not. The spirit world may send cautions and suggestions about the future but never do they tell me exactly what, unquestionably, will happen. Following the information from the spirits and my own intuition, I can sometimes suggest a path that the person may want to take, a course of action that may help a situation. Never will I say, "This will absolutely happen." How can anyone be sure? There are too many variables involved that can change. Life is fluid and each individual's will shifts his or her future and the future of others. Predicting the future is a rather large responsibility for one as small as me. And, I do not mean small in stature (although that would be true) but small compared to the vast intelligence of the universe.

I remember a woman, Sarah, who was given my name by my jeweler. She called imploring me to give her a reading. Since I did not have time to meet with her in the next week, and she did not want to wait, I spoke with her over the phone lines. Immediately her sister appeared to me and told me how she is constantly with Sarah. I described her sister's pigtails, although she was showing herself as a fifty-something year old woman. I conveyed her single marital status, related how she had been the one who had taken care of their father and even told Sarah that she had passed on in Florida. Sarah's sister relayed some other specific and personal information that should have moved Sarah and helped her. But none of this satisfied Sarah.

"Please tell me, will everything be okay?" Sarah pleaded with me.

Sarah pulled at my heartstrings. She was clearly in emotional pain. In my compassion for her on a personal level, I really wanted to say yes it will be okay, but in truth I did not know for sure. So, instead I told her exactly what her sister was communicating. She said that Sarah should think about selling her house and moving to a less expensive state.

"Oh," Sarah squealed, "Will that solve all my problems?"

I told her that I could not say for sure. Maybe, I suggested, it was something that she had to do to get out of her financial rut. She and her husband were responsible for changing their lives and making it better. That was the message. Was she disappointed that I would not commit? Disappointed was an understatement! She kept pushing me to say something definitive. As much as I would have liked to ease her pain, I would not just say something to make her happy. Again, she sought me out to commune with her relative. I did just that; anything else would have been a lie. My job is to be true to myself, the spirit world, the universe and to the person for whom I am relating information.

Also, as do so many other people, I also enjoy being read on occasion. I cannot read myself. A few years ago, a psychic helped to change the course of my life; yet at no point predicted the future. She allowed me to act on suggestion and go for it. This is one of my favorite stories.

But, first I need to set the stage.

I love to meditate in the bathtub. Not only is it relaxing, but water is a conductor of energy both on earth and above. I arrange the room like the Calgon commercial. In the commercial a woman, her eyes closed face up to heaven, is soaking peacefully in a bathtub and is covered in white and pink sparkling bubbles while glowing orange candles cast warmth and comfort, invoking feelings of serenity and peaceful surrender. This is a great commercial to see at the end of a hard day. Truly, it makes one want to go a take a bath. Well, I always have that image in mind when I enter the sacred space of my own bathtub. I fill my tub with fragrant bubble bath and sea salt (very grounding); light candles of different sizes so that the shadows created are uneven and soft, and soak in the warm soothing water while my mind and spirit take flight.

Yet, there is one aspect of my scenario that is a bit different than the commercial; my telephone is placed strategically on the ledge of the tub near my right hand (for easy access!). Hey, I am a mom (the school may call), a wife (my husband may need me), and a healer (I am constantly on call). Beyond all that, I am also very social and love to talk! Okay, that is the real reason. I am human.

Anyway, on this particular day, I am soaking away, deeply mediating, relaxing and allowing my soul to soar. After about fifteen minutes, I recognized that I needed to re-enter the living world and, thus, opened my eyes and grabbed the phone. I began to go through my caller ids for no particular reason, just because that is what I always do. I noticed a call from Nancy; a woman who had helped to teach my son the martial arts about seven years prior. She had only taught Matthew for about two weeks before she moved on to another dojo, so I really did not know her and had never even had a conversation with her. She was one of those people that popped into my life for a brief second and truly left no imprint. Nancy was just a tiny star in a long ago night. Anyway, I checked my voicemail and found that she had not left a message. So there I was soaking away with nothing much else left to do. Curiosity got the better of me and I called back the number. When Nancy picked up I told her who I was and indicated that I was returning her call.

"I am sorry I do not know who you are or why you are calling." She answered perplexed.

I explained that I simply hit redial on my phone so she *must* have called me. She insisted she did not and truly did not have any recollection of who I was. In an attempt to figure out how her telephone number got on my phone, we went through connections we could have, the kids, friends, etc., and fell short of an answer. We lived in different towns, our children did not know each other and we did not share the same friends. In Connecticut, people tend to be a bit clicky and for the most part find friends within their own communities. At times this is a little reminiscent of the book "The Stepford Wives."

However, the fact remained that her number appeared on my phone. When I pressed redial, the number connected to her. We did not know what to think. This was strange but I knew the spirit world was orchestrating something.

So in all my bravado, I insisted to Nancy, "There must be a reason why your number was on my phone and why I had to connect with you. The universe is trying to tell us something. Please, tell me if you can shed some light on the reason why they want us to connect."

Now of course she could have thought that I was a lunatic and hung up. However, she did not do that. Instead, she continued this strange conversation.

"I just opened a healing center in your town," she said.

Bingo, somehow this had to be the connection! I told her that I was a spiritual healer and, although the reason for our connection was still obscure, we recognized it was somewhere in this realm. Still searching for the reason that her number came up on my phone, Nancy went on to say that there was a psychic reader at her place that evening. I acknowledged this but did not commit to seeing the psychic. The conversation ended pleasantly with each of us saying that we would try to come up with a solid reason for the universe pushing us together.

Not being able to hold this information to myself, a couple hours later, I called my friend, Michelle, and told her this strange but interesting story.

"You have to see this psychic tonight. That is the reason for the call. It is right there in front of you." Michelle was rather insistent, as I tried to come up with reasons why this was not a good night for me.

"I will go with you if that is what it takes to get you there. It will be fun. What do you have to lose?"

Well, I thought, I could waste precious time! Yet, Michelle had three children, one being a toddler. If she was willing to rearrange her night for me, I knew I had to go.

"Okay," I acquiesced, "if she has two appointments available, we will go. If the universe wants me there, it will be."

After calling back Nancy, I learned that, miraculously someone had cancelled and two appointments were available! Okay, now I was ready and accepting of the fact that I had to be there, without question. And so, we went. I had no expectations, but my curiosity was peaked. I entered the space where the psychic was doing the readings and was met by a rather large, yet unassuming woman. She was very sweet and soft spoken. I felt very comfortable as she gently recited some prayers and began the reading.

This gifted woman's goal was not to make me happy; not to pretend to predict the future based upon my wishes, but rather to relate to me my path. What struck me was the information was all about getting me on track to fulfill my purpose as a medium; something that I was not doing wholeheartedly at that time.

"Did someone very close to you die last October?" She asked.

"No." I answered.

"Was someone you know on the brink of death during that time?"

I thought for a moment. "No, not that I am aware."

As the words left my mouth and hit the air between us, it struck me. It was me! I had suffered a severe anemic episode the previous October that resulted in a full transfusion and a brief hospital stay. At that time, after months of feeling terrible, my body gave out. Finally, when my heart was palpitating at a rate that was unimaginable, and my breathing was labored as I climbed the stairs to the upper level of my house; when I had to lie down to regain my energy after putting away the laundry, I decided to see my doctor. I had not been doing any Reiki or other healing on myself at the time. I was caught up in the lives of my family. This is not an excuse, and I was taught a powerful lesson about taking care of myself. I am important and it is impossible to take care of everyone else if my health is at stake. This is all reminiscent of the words in so many books on healing, "Healer, heal thyself!" We all have to take care of ourselves. So, when I could not function anymore, off I ventured to my doctor.

The minute my doctor saw me she announced that she was going to call an ambulance to get me to the hospital. I thought she was crazy! She informed me that I was on the verge of a heart attack and did not want me to collapse in her office. Not wanting to upset my children or my husband by the news of their mother and wife being transported to the hospital via ambulance, I decided to drive myself. This is called denial and stupidity. I told you I was a mere, fallible human.

Upon calling my husband at work and telling him of my plan, he rushed home, drove me to the emergency room at the hospital where a team of doctors were waiting for the "severely anemic" woman on the threshold of death. It was like a scene out of one of those medical programs on television. The nurse took a few vials of my blood, which showed a 4.8 hemoglobin level (normal is 12.0!). This is pretty horrible and resulted in a lack of oxygen moving from my blood to the organs of my body and specifically, to my heart. The doctor proceeded to order blood and for the next twenty-four hours blood from a bag hanging next to me was pumped into my veins. At no point was I frightened, nor did I feel like I was checking out of this planet. Yet, apparently I was on my way up to the light. Two years later, after my reading with the psychic, my hematologist asked me if she could use my story as a case study that she was presenting. I laughed and asked her why she thought my story was so unique.

"Because," she explained, "you were minutes, if not seconds from death. Look at you now. You are fine; better than fine. You are healthy!"

After telling the psychic that the person who almost died was me, she explained the reason why I still walk on this earth plane. This explanation was crucial to my life at this time. The psychic calmly went on to relate that my soul did not want to continue with this life, but my physical being could not leave my family. My love for my family overrode the desire to move onto that glorious place beyond us. And so, she said, I made a pact with the universe. On a soul level, my higher self decided that if I were to continue to breathe on this planet, I had to live accepting and using my gifts, and therefore, grow into the healer that I was meant to be. On a soul level, I agreed to acknowledge my gifts and use them in a way that would touch many, many people. This was not a revelation for me. I knew in my heart it to be true. It reverberated deep within the depths of my soul. And so, this suggestion of the path that I should follow ignited the flame in my soul and in my conscious mind to elevate and expand my healing practice. The psychic did not say I would become the greatest medium that ever lived; that is not important to me. Just touching as many people as possible in order to conduct healing is a high enough aspiration.

Based upon the words of this woman, the choice to follow the desire of the universe, and my own higher self, was ultimately my choice. Without missing a beat, my heart chose to respect the path that my soul had agreed to follow when my life was allowed to continue on that fateful October day. In gratitude for my life, I had to give of myself for the harmony and solidarity of the people who walked this plane with me. I had to accept and promote the healer inside of me and allow my gifts to mature. Of course, since I accepted this part of my life, I have hit stumbling blocks along the way, but I view them as teachings. Like everyone else, my path has had its ups and downs but I am doing the best I can and that is the bottom line. My intention is to live, *really live*, the life that I was given.

Once again, at no point did this psychic tell me what would happen. She only relayed what my spirit guides were relating. She proved her credibility by knowing of my illness. She gave me a choice to make that would determine my future. I made the choice and thus, created my own path.

So what am I saying here? You must always be aware that you are the Captain of your own future ship – no one else. You can make or break the deal. And, there are some things out of your control, for instance, which university will accept your child. Some things are a crapshoot. Live your life today. Do not worry about the future; do not live in the future. We miss so much by not being aware of what we have and all the wonderful things around us today. Listen to the radio and the message that come through as songs, or to the cashier in the supermarket who is imparting wisdom that only you understand. Go ahead and plan your future, set your intentions but truly live today.

~Sixteen~

We are All Children of the Universe, Both the Greatest of Teachers and Students.

When the chord of truth is played by the God within it rings the same strings in the neophyte's soul that also vibrated in the teacher, and in an instant they understand each other.
J.J. Dewey

Life has taught me that simultaneously, I am perpetually the student and the teacher. It is a wonderful revelation in that it instills humbleness and gratitude for the information given and received. It creates a natural balance and allows us to share and learn on a daily basis. I am not an all-knowing guru; I am just a woman living her life to the best of her ability. My road has had thorns and beautiful, sweet smelling roses. Yet, like everyone I can be stubborn and, dare I say, human!

Recently a friend, who was also one of my students, complained to me that I referred to her as my student in the presence of many people. I apologized to her for my apparent, yet unintended, insult. But her reaction to my words bothered me, and after giving it much thought, I came to the conclusion that we were both at fault in our thinking. Our egos came into play in a way that defied the intention of the words and the meaning behind them. My ego wanted credit for this woman's wonderful healing work. I, as her teacher, felt a bit of responsibility in her journey and on some level wanted the recognition for a part in her success. My ego in its monster state blew up and indirectly was taking credit for her spiritual success. How narcissistic! How arrogant! How human. On her part, her ego said, "I am not the student! How degrading! I cannot be the student; I am the master." Her ego personified, stood with chest out as well, displaying arrogance and narcissism. We were both being human and projecting our ego. The bottom line is that we are all students and teachers as we go through this life and, from what the spirits convey, into the spiritual realm as well.

It is interesting how the universe fortifies our reasoning and thinking and brings us back on track when we stray in our thoughts. Often, when I am teaching, my students begin to see blue jays or bluebirds in their daily lives. I am often followed by cardinals and sometimes by the blue birds as well. Upon research into the symbolic meaning of these birds as totem animals, I learned that the blue bird is symbolic of the student and the cardinal of the teacher. One of my students told me that right after my class a blue jay had gotten stuck under her porch. Mmmm, in helping the bird out, was she symbolically releasing the student who was housed within herself? Who ever said the universe was subtle? Not always. Others have relayed incidents of many cardinals literally flying into the windshields of their cars or the windows and screens of their homes. Again, do you recognize the teacher? Let her in! And who is the teacher? Given all the bluebird and cardinal sightings, I decided to really explore the meaning of these birds for all of us and came across the following Native American story. Let the story sink in deeply. We are all the sharers of information and the receivers – the teachers and the students. We should be proud to be both.

Noquisi and the Bird
(By Takatoka) ©1994-2006
(Reprinted with permission of the Manataka American Indian Council. http://www.manataka.org/page294.html)

It is said a long time ago there was an unhappy young girl named Noquisi (which means Star) who lived among the Kituwah (Cherokee) deep in the Blue Mountains. Noquisi's sadness was not understood by her mother and father as they were loving and kind parents who provided little Noquisi with plenty of food, good shelter and lovely clothing.

Noquisi had many cousins and friends with which to play but instead she would wander off by herself to sit at the edge of the forest and cry. Her playmates had decided Noquisi did not like them and they began to dislike her. In the family lodge, Noquisi was quarrelsome and found disfavor with everyone and almost everything. Even the drumming and dancing during time of ceremony did not cheer up the sad little Noquisi. No one knew why Noquisi was sad, not even herself. She loved her mother and father and knew they wished for her to be happy, but she was sad anyway. She knew her cousins and friends were starting to dislike her, but there was nothing she could do about her sadness.

Noquisi was a kind and gentle girl and she loved her animal friends. She once enjoyed imitating little bird cousins, but the pleasure of singing with the birds left her a long time ago. Sadly, she did not know how to get it back again. Her miserable feelings were deep and con-fused. Sometimes, she was so sad that she thought about throwing herself off a mountain or running away into the forest to be eaten by Odalv Wesa (Mountain Lion). Noquisi was very sad and confused.

Then one day as Noquisi sat under a large white oak tree, the spirit of Edoda (God) spoke softly to her. "Noquisi, you may leave the world if that is your desire, but you must first go to the waters and make a Gasaqualv Etikaiele (Sacred Circle) and point a finger out in front of you."

Noquisi was stunned; never before had the Spirit spoken to her. At first she was frightened, and then as she thought about the words the Spirit spoke, she doubted her own mind and whispered to herself, "This cannot be. I am only a little girl and I do not know how to build a sacred circle." Spirit then spoke again saying, "Noquisi, you must go to the waters and make a circle. Stand in the center of the circle, close your eyes and hold a finger in front of you. You will be shown the way."

Noquisi sat silently under the tree in shock. It was getting late when she arose from deep thought and decided to go back to the village so her mother and father would not worry. On the way, she came to the trail that led to the nearby lake. Standing in the middle of both trails, she again thought about the words of the Spirit and turned down the lake trail forgetting that it was getting dark and her parents concern.

Noquisi quickly found a perfect place between two giant willows beside the lake to build a circle. She gathered forty-nine stones and carefully placed each one around the circle. She cleaned the inside of lose twigs and debris and stood in the middle of the circle surveying her work. Without thinking, she did what Spirit told her to do. She closed her eyes and pointed a finger in front of her.

A few seconds later, Noquisi felt a little tickle on her finger and opened her eyes with a silent gasp. There stood a red bird perched on her finger." Hello Noquisi, I am Red Bird" said the bird. Noquisi quickly shut her eyes again and felt like running home, but she was frozen in disbelief and wonder. It was now dark and she thought she may be imagining things out of fear. As she slowly opened her eyes again, the bird still sat on her extended finger." Hello Noquisi, I am here to help you, to guide you on the path of your destiny. If you leave the world your destiny will not happen."

Staring in disbelief at little Red Bird, tears came to her eyes as she realized this was not a dream and she was not imagining that a bird had just spoken to her. Many thoughts raced through her mind as she tried to comprehend what Red Bird had just said. Feelings of great joy finally emerged from Noquisi's heart as she realized this was really happening. She knew it was a message from Edoda who was saying a destiny awaited her. All the sad feelings of being lost and alone left her in an instant. Wiping tears from her eyes, she and Red Bird quietly talked for a long time in the sacred circle.

As Grandmother Moon emerged from behind a cloud and the stars of the heavens shined brightly, the loving and wise words of Red Bird penetrated her mind and heart. Listening intently to every word, Noquisi barely noticed when a commotion in the woods was filtering through her consciousness. Then she realized it was her family who were looking for her. As the sound of their voices calling her name grew closer, she was fearful that Red Bird would fly away and she would never see him. At that moment, Red Bird disappeared but out of the mist hanging over the lake she heard, "Do not fear Noquisi, we will talk again. I will never leave you. Return to this place and hold out your finger and I will appear."

Noquisi turned around to see her father and cousins enter the clearing. "There you are!" they shouted." It is time to be in the lodge", said her father as he sternly took her hand and led her home. Part way down the path, Noquisi tugged on her father's hand and stopped to face him. Looking up she said, "I love you Father", with a smile on her face. Father said, "I love you too daughter", as they continued walking down the path home. Father thought to himself that it was the first time he had seen a smile on his daughter's face in a long, long time.

From that time on, Noquisi came to her special place by the lake every day, making sure to return before dark. She brought small offerings of food for her new friend. Red Bird always appeared and gifted Noquisi with many lessons. She carefully listened as the bird reminded her that she had the power to make changes in her life. He told her about the mysteries of life and wonderful blessings she was given. They spoke about tough changes she needed to make in her life and the mountains of troubles she must endure in the future. At the end of each visit as the mist rose on the lake, Noquisi bid farewell to Red Bird and she performed a little thank you prayer ceremony in the sacred circle.

Changes began to take place in Noquisi's life. She was no longer quarrelsome with her family and friends. She happily greeted her cousins and friends each day and gave them many gifts she had made from materials gathered during visits to the forest. Mother and Father were very happy. Noquisi grew in many ways during the next two seasons.

Then one day Noquisi decided to make a special gift for Red Bird as thanks for his many lessons. Arriving early at her special place by the lake, Noquisi gathered small limbs and twigs from the willow trees and carefully peeled the bark to expose the reddish skin. Then she fashioned a birdhouse with a comfortable nest inside. Entering the circle she closed her eyes and extended her finger.

Red Bird immediately appeared and Noquisi happily showed her gift saying, "This is a gift in exchange for the wonderful things you have given to me."

The bird reacted by saying, "My friend, I have given you nothing that you did not have already. My purpose has been to show you ways to see within yourself and to make you understand that the power to change things comes from within. The people around you have not changed, but you changed the way you look at life. Look into this lake. Do you see the reflection of your face? You must always search for what is beneath the surface of that reflection into the depths of your soul."

With that, Red Bird disappeared and never returned again.

Noquisi spent many hours by the lake between the willow trees, sitting inside her sacred circle, waiting for Red Bird to return." Red Bird said he would never leave me" she remembered. Knowing there must be a good answer for his disappearance, she chose instead to dwell on all the good lessons the bird taught. She learned to trust her inner feelings and disregard negative thoughts of the mind. She loved her dear little friend and wanted to ask him a thousand questions, but as she peered deeply into the lake waters, she found strength and pondered at length on ways she could use those precious words in her life.

As time went by, Noquisi grew into a fine woman and leader among her people. Noquisi became an important healer helping many of her nation and people of other tribes to use their inner-power to make positive changes for themselves and others. She was well-known throughout the Blue Mountains as a peacemaker and wise elder. She became a teacher and regularly took on new students to tutor in the medicine ways. Noquisi used what was in her heart to guide them.

Noquisi's answers to the problems of her people came from within her because she never forgot what Red Bird had taught. When she was not involved in the affairs of the nation, Noquisi found time to improve her childhood ability to imitate the song birds. She spent many hours twilling and chirping their language and improving their habitat. As an old woman Noquisi became known as the "Bird Woman" because she had perfected the calls and songs of every bird in the Blue Mountains. It was a name she loved to hear spoken. Her hair and clothing was adorned with feathers. Her lodge became home and sanctuary to many bird species. She learned the powers and gifts of all the bird people. She never forgot to give thanks to the wonderful gift as she walked with the spirit of the bird.

Noquisi's neighbors and relatives, especially her grand-children, love to visit her lodge. Nestled in the clearing between two giant hickory trees overlooking the lake of her childhood, Noquisi's lodge was completely covered with flowering vines and honeysuckle that made perfect cover for the nests of many types of birds. It was the perfect home for people and birds. It always seemed curious to Noquisi that no red birds had ever visited her home. But, she knew their nature was to be among their own kind and they did not like being in large communities of other birds.

One early morning a student of Bird Woman's, Tsi-quo-quo Sagonigi (Blue Robin) came for another lesson. Blue Robin was the most faithful and attentive among all her students and a special bond had developed between Noquisi and Blue Robin. It seemed the connection between the two went far beyond their understanding. When the student sat quietly at her feet, Noquisi always felt Blue Robin was looking deep into her soul. On this morning, they went to the sacred circle by the lake as part of their normal ritual in preparation of the day's activities. They closed their eyes and began offering prayers of thanks.

As they opened their eyes again, a red bird quickly flitted past their vision into the woods beyond. "Oh my", exclaimed Noquisi, "that is the first time I have seen a red bird here by the lake in many years!

Blue Robin looked curiously at her mentor and said, "But teacher, what about the red bird that is always sitting on your shoulder?"

The words of her insightful student grabbed her heart and shook her deep inside. Noquisi felt faint and moved to sit down at the edge of the lake. In an instant, many years of questions were answered. All the old fears she worked so hard to bury inside were gone. At last, everything in creation made sense; her life's struggles and successes were made clear. Her destiny was fulfilled.

Noquisi peered into the lake and remembered the day when Red Bird did not return and realized he really never left and had been whispering into her ear all these many years. A joy of untold depth welled up inside her as tears streamed down her cheek.

At that moment, Red Bird appeared in reflection on the surface of the lake and once again spoke to her." Yes Noquisi, I told you that Red Bird would never leave you and I have not. On the day I did not appear on your finger and instead lit on your shoulder, you had a choice. You could have returned to being sad and miserable. Or, you could have waited for me in vain hoping my guidance would answer your every question in life. Instead, you decided to heed my words. You reminded yourself that I could not give you what you already had inside yourself. You knew the power was within to make the changes needed. You knew that healing begins and ends deep within your heart and soul. I am very proud of you. You have completed your higher purpose on earth and given much to the sacred circle *of life. Now you know that Spirit is not separate from the person. We Are One."*

This is a story about assimilating Spirit into one's life. It is a story about opening ones eyes to the knowledge that every heart knows from birth. The moral of this story has been taught for millenniums by our ancient grandfathers and grandmothers. And so it is…

Yes, and so it is, and so it will be. Go on with your life and allow the universe to teach you through others, and be prepared to pass on your knowledge to those around you. Keep your eyes and ears open to knowledge and allow your heart to speak your truth and share the wonderful person that you have grown to be.

Part II:

Making the Connection

For to one is given through the Spirit the utterance of wisdom, and to another the utterance of knowledge according to the same Spirit, to another faith by the same Spirit, to another gifts of healing by the one Spirit, to another the working of miracles, to another prophecy, to another the ability to distinguish between spirits, to another various kinds of tongues, to another the interpretation of tongues.

I Corinthians 12:8-10
(<u>English Standard Version</u> Bible)

~Seventeen~

So You Want to Talk to the Spirit World . . .

When you live in surrender, something comes through you into the world of duality that is not of this world.
Eckhart Tolle

Everything you'll ever need to know is within you; the secrets of the universe are imprinted on the cells of your body. But you haven't learned how to read the wisdom of the body.
Dan Millman

I believe that everyone can converse with the universe and the spirit world. It may not be in the way that I do, but you certainly can do it in your way. We, as a race, have not even come close to touching on our many gifts. As it is, research has shown that we only use ten percent of our brain. If you desire to open up your intuitive side, it will take some practice and perhaps some behavior modifications that will be unique to your own spirit. Many people have asked how I go about communicating with those on the other side. I would be honored to share that part of me with you. You may be able to learn and use some of the techniques with which I have learned to rely upon over the years. Perhaps this discussion may spark an image of what you should be doing to open up your heart to the universe and accept and use your own gifts. Remember, the gifts of the spirit are personal to each one of us and unveiled when the time is perfect for us to accept them. Many people become impatient or feel they are not worthy. If you are not feeling the connection, it simply may not be your time; do not give up. Rather, surrender your ego, and permit the mystery of your gifts to be revealed to you. Be conscious of the minute details and capitalize on the beauty that blossoms in your heart.

The key to connection with the other side is to put the "me" aside and converse with the heavenly realm directly through the soul and heart. Like all conversations, it is a balancing act between listening and speaking, asking and receiving. It is being in the moment and only in that particular moment, ready and willing to hear the voice of the universe speaking loudly and clearly. Most of us have been taught to recite the prayers of our religion, but do you really know how to give your heart and soul to Divinity? Do you know how to be still and empty yourself? It is essential to become an open vessel, a hollow bone, as the Native American shamans like to say. In order for the information to be pure and unadulterated, it must be unfiltered and unaffected by your own ego. This can be done in a variety of ways.

Keep this practice simple. There is no need to complicate it. Conversing with the universe is a natural act for which we are programmed. Keep yourself humble and willing to hear whatever may come through to you. In this practice, it is essential to live your life in total wakefulness. You must go through your days and nights being aware and conscious of what you see and hear. Therefore, you must walk your walk with your eyes and ears engaged, not just existing and going through the motions as we are all so apt to do. It is also important to be in constant conversation with God, your spirit guides, and the entire heavenly realm. Place yourself in a constant state of communication. The line between you and the spirit world must always be an open portal. This is not a perfect science, and we are not perfect beings. Yet, in the midst of our imperfection and fallibility there must always be a sense of being surrounded by the almighty Power.

In the following chapters, are descriptions of the ways in which I have learned to connect to heaven. I hope that these techniques help you on your own quest for spiritual growth. Take from it what works for you and propels you on your own personal journey.

~Eighteen~

Walking Through Life with Eyes Wide Open

*You can become blind by seeing each day as
a similar one. Each day is a different one;
each day brings a miracle of its own. It's just
a matter of paying attention to this miracle.*
Paul Coelhoe

We live in a hectic world. As we race from here to there,
we sometimes miss the phenomenal happenings along the
way. We become unfocused as we move through the routine
of our lives. We only perceive that which is in front of us;
our peripheral vision is cut off. We all need to take off the
blinders and really see the world and the all the wonderful
things it has in store for us.

Think about it. How many times have we arrived at our
destination, driving to work, the supermarket or wherever we
drive on a regular basis, not having a recollection of the
mechanics of the drive or what we passed along the way?
Are we hearing what is being played on the radio or is it just
background noise? We pass people, buildings, animals and

yes, spirits along the way and do not give them any attention. If a spirit yelled your name through the radio, would that get your attention? In order to grow, we need to live consciously and be aware of everything in our world.

By doing so, it may seem as if the universe is expanding as it infiltrates our lives. The little things start to excite us as we recognize their importance. Seeing a hawk swooping down for the third time in one day becomes not just an animal in flight, barely inside our field of vision, but something far greater. We might pause and try to figure out what the universe is trying to communicate as we give thought to what the hawk represents symbolically for us. It is then that those on the other side applaud for you and for themselves. They can find their way in to communicate; your eyes are open.

If really living life and being one with the universe is your choice, then do not wait any longer. The time to start is now. It is simple; just be conscious. Do not complicate it. Just allow all your senses and your mind to engage in all that is around you. Open your eyes; really open your conscious-ness, and marvels will manifest for you.

Moreover, it is important not to pick and choose the things of which you want to be aware. Just live and be cognizant of everything that you possibly can and search for the meanings in what you see and hear. You might hear a song on the radio that touches you on a soul level or lyrics that move you; think about the words and what they mean to you. When you "coincidently" think of an old friend and the phone rings and it's her, think about the bigger picture and the reason behind the call. It is all there for you to ponder. As we go through these motions mindfully, we grow at a speed that is incomprehensible. The universe recognizes our need to explore our own souls and rises up to the challenge to help us along. It is pretty powerful. The more we stop rushing around, the more we can live; the more we live, the more we see beyond our normal existence into the heavenly realm. So, what are you waiting for? Stop rushing around; open your eyes; question what you see, hear and feel and, and start to live.

~Nineteen~

Meditation - The Transition from Head to Heart

Meditation is the dissolution of thoughts in Eternal awareness or pure consciousness without objectification, knowing without thinking, merging finitude in infinity.
Swami Sivananda

The best way to enter your zone, the place where the spirit world communicates with you, is to actually find your zone; feel it and recognize it. Once you have entered into it even once, you can enter it again and again.

Meditation is a great way to settle your mind and move into your heart. If you meditate and can clear your mind; you will be transported and lifted to another level of your being. You feel it deep within the pit of your stomach as you are lifted to the consciousness of the universe. It is as though you turn off the lights in one part of yourself and flick on a switch that illuminates another dimension of you. Your reality shifts and so does your consciousness. Try it. I am not proposing that you will immediately connect to the spirit world. I do not know if that is your path. Maybe you need to connect to your higher self, or another gift of healing. Your soul knows what you need; not what you want, but what you need. Therefore, allow yourself to be led by the Spirit.

Meditation takes practice and patience. If you have never meditated before, it may be difficult to reach a meditative state immediately. Take what you get and let it grow as time moves on. Do not be hard on yourself. The biggest challenge is stilling the "Monkey Chatter", as it is sometimes called, in our minds. Unlike some other places in the world, in the United States people are taught to think and think and then think some more. It seems that we just cannot stop thinking! The best way to train your mind to rest, is when a thought enters, simply acknowledge it, respect it and say that you will think about it later. After some time, this will train your mind to wait until you are finished meditating to release all the chatter. Please do not beat yourself up, or become discouraged. Keep practicing and always be grateful for the strides that you make.

Another difficulty faced by those who desire to incorporate meditation into their lives is time. We live in a culture where time is dear. Americans are on a constant time schedule; we are always looking at the clock. Whether we are running off to the office, taking our children to their various activities, cooking, cleaning or even going to the gym; we are on a tight schedule with thoughts racing through our heads at an impressive speed. But, if we have at least fifteen minutes a day; we can meditate. Of course, the more time you devote to meditating, the greater your rewards. If you are just beginning, start small with small amounts of time and let the time expand as you mature in your practice. And be patient.

Thus, meditation, for Americans, includes a semi-behavior modification. We must reprogram ourselves to be still and not think — not to be on guard. The benefits of meditation and going beyond our thoughts to the stillness of our souls are great and your higher self will promote your growth. Make time for meditation and give it a priority status – the dishes can wait thirty minutes, television time can be cut by a half hour, etc. Please do not take time from your family; they are a precedent and the universe supports that, but there are so many other activities that are not essential to your life. And, please, please do not punish yourself or become stressed if you cannot stick to your own preordained scheduled time to meditate. It is not about self-recrimination, but about spiritual connectedness and growth; anything else is counterproductive.

Following are some suggestions to help you get started on your meditative practice, or to help you work out the kinks in your established practice.

Find your sacred space. It is essential to find a place that is sacred to you. By sacred I mean a place where you feel a sense of comfort and spirituality. It does not have to be a church or a temple; rather, it should be a place that you can get to at any given time. You should try to find a place in your home or very nearby, maybe directly outside in nature. Your sacred space could be in a cozy room in your house, on your porch, sitting on your lawn or even in your bathroom! It does not matter.

A friend of mine wakes up at 5:00 a.m., before her husband and children start their day, stumbles into her walk-in closet, puts down a "prayer rug" and meditates. This is her sacred place and her special time to commune with the universe. It works for her. Be patient, cut yourself a break and find what works best for you. There is no right or wrong; it is about what place and time allows your spirit to glide and connect. While connecting to your higher self and the universal realm, you must be in a quiet space, away from the hustle and bustle of family life, with the television, radio, as well as the ringer on your telephone, turned off. Find a comfortable chair or place to sit and ease yourself into a state of tranquility.

I like to meditate in my living room. It is my room. I do not hold classes or healing sessions in this space. Except on holidays when we entertain, no one really uses the living room but me. The room has lots of windows from which stream rays of light — yellow, blue and white — bringing a spiritual aliveness to the space. I sit on the same sofa in the same position each and every time I meditate. It is my sacred space. To someone else, it may appear to be just a living room, but to me it is far more.

Surround yourself with your "sacred stuff." Also, it helps to bring your "sacred stuff" into the space. For instance, you may have a crystal that you love; a statute that you feel connects you to heaven; a prayer or meditation rug; a special piece of jewelry or a candle. Whatever you feel will support the holiness of your space should surround you. It could be one object, or it could be many. Whatever works for you and helps to bring comfort and the feeling of heaven and peace into your world. Using the same props each time you meditate will help to set the tone and to reinforce the sacredness of the ritual.

One of your sacred objects should be a meditation journal. This journal can be a notebook or a journal that you can pick up in any variety store but should be used solely for journaling before and after you meditate. At the beginning of the meditation, you may want to write down a question to be answered by the universe while you are meditating. Directly afterwards, write down all your thoughts, images, words that you may hear and everything about the meditation. This practice of journaling is very important for remembering what the spirits are dictating to you as well as to view and acknowledge the progression of the growth of your higher self. In time, you may be able to record what you see, feel and hear as it is happening. Yet, for the here and now wait until your meditation is complete to jot down what you may. You must allow yourself approximately five minutes to write it all in the journal. It is not necessary to write in full sentences (unless that makes you happy), but rather just jot down the essential aspects of what you see, hear and feel. This is for you. Again, do what is best for you personally.

Meditate during the same time each day. Pick a time during the day or night during which you are less likely to be interrupted. I know this is difficult if you have small children, just do the best you can. I also recognize how difficult this can be at the end of a hard day at work, but it is very important that you find the time. Again, even if it is fifteen minutes, just do it! If music calms you, play a continuous music track that relaxes you. Do not play music with lyrics that you can get caught up in. There are so many meditative musical compositions to choose from, you should not have any problem finding something that you can relate to on a soul level. Many of the music stores allow you to sample the music before you purchase. I-tunes is also a wonderful place to purchase and download music. Experiment with different music and find what calms you and brings you to a new level of awareness.

Clear your sacred space and protect yourself. Each time you enter your sacred space to meditate, you should clear the space of all negative energy. Sit in a comfortable position and image a blazing white light filling every corner of the room in purifying love. As this white light fills the room, ask God to dispel any negativity. You may see darkness leaving as the bright light of heaven replaces it. As you imagine the light, feel it enveloping the entire room in its warmth. Feel the white light moving through the room and through your body making you and the energy of the room one with the universal energy. See it; feel it. Petition God and his angelic realm to protect you and the space where you are meditating. Allow yourself to breath in the goodness and light.

Without question, it is very important, prior to meditation and opening yourself up to the universe, to protect yourself from any negativity that may try to make its way into your body. There are many ways in which to accomplish this. If you have a technique that you like and have been using, continue. I like to use the simplest way possible. Do not try to complicate this procedure — the more effortless, the better.

Prior to beginning your meditation, and just after asking for the room to be protected, imagine a white bubble, or cocoon, surrounding your entire body. With your eyes closed, see this white light encasing you. Ask for it to protect you during your meditation and throughout your day and night. Feel the protection and know that it is keeping out all negative forces. Thank the universe for the dispelling of all negative energy and thoughts during this time of quiet introspection.

You can also image this bubble of protection around your family and friends. I sheath Vinny as he goes off to work and my sons as they leave for school. This protection does not mean our days will be perfect, but it does block negative energy from entering our auras and our bodies.

Once you are protected, you are ready to lose yourself to the universe. Do not put any pressure on yourself. Meditation is so basic that it defies logic, and we as human beings struggle with its lack of complexity. We are taught to see beyond the simple instead of just accepting it for what it is. Our minds are always working, always seeking the answers while our egos are forever controlling and fighting for control. Meditation is the practice that moves us beyond these trappings of our psyche and the culture in which we live. In all its simplicity, people struggle with quieting their minds.

Be conscious of your breathing. Breathing is the key to being able to meditate. It is the life force that moves us and transports us to a "non-ordinary" reality. While breathing, we take in the essence of the Spirit. The word, Spirit, is derived from the Latin word Spiritus, means breath. With that in mind, it is important to breathe deeply and fully, moving your breath from your abdomen up through your sternum and lungs and exhaling from your mouth. Concentrate on your breathing; allow each inhalation to move through your torso and fill your lungs, while releasing the stress and tension of the day with each exhale. As you relax your body and mind, distance yourself from the motions and moments of your morning or afternoon, and concentrate on the present moment. As you follow this prescription and become immersed in a state of relaxation, remain conscious of your surroundings as your spirit, the essence of your being, ascends to its full height, rising out of your body and connecting to the matrix of the universe.

With your eyes closed, as you focus on your breathing, imagine your breath as a white cloud entering your feet and moving up your body to your crown and connecting you to a higher realm. See it, feel it. Continue to breathe as you feel each part of your body giving way to relaxation. As the tension leaves your body, feel yourself drifting as you continue to breathe deeply. Permit the toxins that you carry to float away with each breath as they are replaced with Divine energy and strength. Breathe, breathe, and breathe some more. When you are totally relaxed, and your breathing has taken precedence over your mind chatter, you are ready to connect to the heavenly realm.

~Twenty~

Can You Hear Me? I Am Listening.

In the midst of movement and chaos, keep stillness inside of you.
Deepak Chopra

If you have not taken your blinders off already, now would be a good time. In order to converse with the universe, you must see, feel and hear with every piece of your being. It is essential to walk your path always plugged in and connected in some way to the other side. If this becomes your modus operandi, connecting during meditation is a cinch. Once again, it is about being mindful and aware as we go about our daily routine. It is important to be in a state of perpetual dialogue with the heavenly realm. If speaking to heaven and listening to the responses from the other side becomes a way of living, then turning on the conversation while mediating will be natural. When you are at ease and familiar with being able to talk to heaven, those on the other side will use their energy to move into your awareness and converse with you. Keep talking! Keep listening! And, more importantly pay attention to the conversation around you. The dead speak volumes in sometimes unconventional ways.

As a medium, and as a spiritual being on this planet, I am always connecting above and constantly hearing and feeling the voices from beyond. Over the centuries, people have struggled with the dynamics of speaking to God. Many of us battle our demons, and feel that our words may not be worthy enough for the ears of the Divine. Maybe, we think that our end of the conversation should be eloquent, refined and perfect in the words we chose. We fail to recognize that God and the universe do not judge us on the words, but on the sincerity of heart. The goal in speaking to heaven is to open up your heart and let genuine feeling and truth, whatever it may be, reach the heavens. For those of us who relish in the art of "socializing" this can be an uncomplicated and fun endeavor. Constantly "socializing" and chit chatting with the universe brings us into a continual state of unity.

So, what really is this conversation? Is this prayer? And, what really is prayer? It's just a label for the simple act of entering into a spiritual communion with God and the universe through conversation. It is the ability to bear our hearts and souls, our deepest fears, desires and pain, as well as, our gratitude and joy for the many gifts and pleasures we derive in this life. It is just talking and saying what is on our minds at any given point. Prayer is a private link between each person and his God and the universe and is defined by that individual relationship. Prayer is natural when it comes from your inner sanctum. And, when you allow yourself to actually feel your prayer and become one with it, you know that you are loved without question or pause. Prayer brings you into the arms of the Divine. It is here that the profound magnitude of comfort and safety will allow the seedlings of the gifts of your spirit to germinate.

Therefore, our conversations with the universe form a prayer as our sincerity of heart unfolds and is laid before the heavens while we accept the other side of the conversation into our hearts. Genuine prayer is pure and unadulterated, has no bounds, no limitations and does not question motivation. Moreover, at its highest pinnacle, it is a bond, a golden cord from our hearts to the Heart of the heavens; a heart that bears no judgment and surrounds us with unconditional love. Prayer is by its very nature a balancing act — a task of "give and take." Its two-sided nature implies respect and love. The Buddhists would appropriately maintain that in every facet of our lives there must be balance in order for us to reach a state of equilibrium in mental, emotional and spiritual health. So, this two-way exchange of ideas, thoughts and feelings between us and heaven establishes this balance and propels us further into our own spirituality.

It is easy and uncomplicated. If you can speak to your friends, your spouse, your mother, your children or the wide array of people with whom you come in contact with everyday, you certainly can speak to God. And, by the same token, if you can quiet your own voice and listen to the voices of other people, you can reach the level of quieting your mind and allowing yourself to hear the Voice as it whispers into your heart and breathes into your soul. If you are like me, you can and will hear, see, smell and touch the very presence of the universe, as God and those on the other side tap you on your shoulders and drum their fingers lightly on your heart.

One of the most important aspects of prayer is that it is authentic. God knows you too well; you cannot fool Him. Therefore, in my case, in the less than reverent style of speaking that I call my own; He hears me. He knows me. There is no reason to make myself sound like the holier-than-thou person that I certainly am not. I must speak my own language and let my heart sing its own song in order to be me. Mark Twain's character Huck Finn in The Adventures of Huckleberry Finn, illustrates the importance of sincerity in prayer when he says,

It made me shiver, and I about made up my mind to pray and see if I could not try to quit being' the kind of boy I was and be better. So I kneeled down. But the words wouldn't come. Why wouldn't they? It were not no use to try and hide it from Him...I knowed very well why they wouldn't come. It was because my heart was not right; it was because I was playin' double. I was lettin' on to give up sin, but way inside of me I was holdin' on to the biggest one of all. I was tryin' to make my mouth say I would do the right thing and the clean thing, but deep down in me I knowed it was a lie and He knowed it. You cannot pray a lie. I found that out.

As difficult as it may be, it is essential to push away the ego and allow the soul, pure and simple, to be humbled before a greater Power.

Give thanks. At the beginning of my meditations, I always give thanks. It is always important to express gratitude to the universe. Expressions of gratitude acknowledge that all good is somehow related to the Divine. As I meditate, as my body becomes more relaxed, I thank God for all the blessings in my life. In my own words, I thank the higher Power for the gifts bestowed upon me and humble myself as my ego is pushed aside. I become small next to the all encompassing Power. I offer up my soul and my person to the heavens in praise. My discourse is simple and I silently speak as I would with anyone standing or sitting before me. You can just say "thanks" or you can choose to enumerate your blessings. Whatever feels right for you personally; whatever your heart commands is the course you should follow. Remember to just be who you are – let your soul fly with your words.

Petition the heavens. There are always things in life that are beyond our control, or experiences that we feel we cannot handle alone. Sometimes, no matter how much others try to help us, or when we feel there is no one to turn to, the very act of turning to God is healing. It is a matter of succumbing and recognizing that we are powerless in the face of human adversity. The very act of asking for help symbolizes and distinguishes between the superiority of God and our human inadequacy. It is both humbling and astonishing that we are so small in the presence of this Power. When I feel that life is overwhelming me, when chaos is settling in and disturbing my spirit, I render it all to God. When I reach the point when I feel helpless, I give all my troubles, especially any mental or emotional pain, up to heaven. I know, that in doing so, Grace will fill the void that once housed my anguish and allow me to unload my stuff in order to hear those on the other side. Grace is a cool, soothing balm that eases the sting of the pain. Unburdening yourself of your problems and all the tension that accompanies them, will allow you to be the "hollow bone." When the pain is released, it permits the voice of the universe to come through loud and clear.

In my experience, visualization brings a new dimension to my meditations. By using my imagination to visualize the release of my troubles, I am able to *see* my prayer in my mind's eye. This enables me to walk through the motions in my mind and see and feel the release of my troubles. I usually visualize my troubles wrapped and tied up in a linen bundle. I imagine myself meandering toward a cliff. When I reach the edge, and there is nowhere else to go, I throw my bundle over the precipice, into the wind and vastness, confident that they will be caught in the arms of God. This can be a very powerful tool. When you feel as though you cannot go on much further it can be cathartic to throw it all away to the willing arms of God. Of course, you can conjure up images that are meaningful to you. Whatever images you choose, the act of surrendering your troubles to God, allows your faith to flourish and the wounds to heal.

Ask for what your heart desires. If you want to use your gifts more fully, ask. By the very act of asking, you are acknowledging that you are only the vehicle; you have no control over these gifts except to accept them and use them. It puts your ego aside and allows you to give yourself up fully to a higher power. When you have concluded the active part of the conversation it is time to listen.

Be silent and listen. Sit in the silence and be conscious of the present moment, the beating of your heart and your breathing.

When all thoughts are pushed out of my mind, I feel a downy-like fluffiness surrounding my body and my heart. I am swathed, enveloped and embraced in an emotion, so big and great that it seems tangible. At times, I have actually reached out my hand to touch it. It is that real. To me, this is the manifestation of pure love. In response to this feeling, my heart starts to palpitate more vigorously, and a warm soothing flush will consume my body as I sit in communion with my God, with Pure Love. And it is at this time that I can hear the universe, my spirit guides and the spirits of those on the other side speak to me. I know these voices are not my own as unfamiliar thoughts gently glide through my consciousness. Often, the emotions that careen through my body speak to my soul when words are not enough. Not only do I feel and hear, but at times, I can even smell the delicate fragrance of certain flowers as the sensations wash over me, flooding my senses.

During this part of the meditation you are the receiver. Capture whatever wonderful feelings, thoughts, images and words that arrive on the door step of your heart. It may take some practice for you to be confident that the voice you are hearing and the sensations you are experiencing are not your own. Relax and just let the experience overtake you and evolve in the way that it is best for you. The simple sense of peace and stillness can be a monumental achievement.

161

Simply acknowledge the feelings and welcome them. Whatever you experience may propel you to yearn to remain in that moment for eternity and reach out for the experience more frequently. After some time you will recognize the feeling of reaching a deep state of meditation and being able to receive. You will begin to communicate with those on the other side more vividly and in your own unique way. This is only the beginning.

Be grateful. When you are ready to leave your meditation behind, thank the universe and the Divine for the energy and love bestowed upon you. Allow yourself to slowly reenter your physical space.

Journal. As mentioned previously, write down whatever you have experienced, whatever words you heard, feelings you felt or anything else that entered your awareness during your meditative state. No matter how ridiculous or silly your thoughts and feelings may be, do not judge them. Sometimes the meanings will be apparent, other times it will take time to figure out the gist of them.

In summary:

- ❖ *Find your sacred space*
- ❖ *Surround yourself with your sacred stuff*
- ❖ *Meditate during the same time each day*
- ❖ *Clear your sacred space and protect yourself*
- ❖ *Be conscious of your breathing*
- ❖ *Give thanks*
- ❖ *Petition the heavens*
- ❖ *Be silent and listen*
- ❖ *Be grateful*
- ❖ *Journal*

You are on your way to entering a world that will never cease to astound you.

~Twenty-One~

Until We Meet Again

May the road rise up to meet you, may the wind be ever at your back. May the sun shine warm upon your face and the rain fall softly on your fields. And until we meet again, may God hold you in the hollow of his hand.
Irish Blessing

As I mentioned in the beginning of this book, I wrote this book out of love. It has been an intense, introspective labor of love in the highest degree. I hope you were able to find a common ground amidst my words and feel my love as well as the love of the universe coming through. It is not about religion; each religion and belief system has its place. In your uniqueness as a member of this planet, your belief system belongs to you and is a facet of your personality as well as your soul. Whatever you believe, believe it with all your heart and soul. The passion of our beliefs pushes us forward and the universe smiles. We do not have to be perfect; we are all fallible and flawed, but we can strive for communion with God and the sharing in this perfect love.

Again and again, the circle goes around and it comes back to love.

The spirits on the other side are attracted to this love. It is like a magnet to a piece of shiny, silver metal. They are pulled toward your compassion and the love you have for them. It because of this love that they use their energy to reenter our world to help heal us or just to say that they love us. It does not get better than that.

So, beyond all else, we should all strive to love and to love deeply. Not just our families, but also those outside of our intimate communities and comfort zones. Love each other. When we can love our fellow human beings, we can truly reach the state of loving ourselves and thus, finding the Divine within each of our hearts and souls. Imagine . . . Heaven would be on earth.

Go on with your life and live each moment, love with a passion, find your dream and talk to those on the other side of the veil.

Works Cited

<u>Contact</u>. Dir: by Robert Zemeckis. Prod. by Lynda Rosen Obst. Writ.by Carl Sagan. Perf. by Jodie Foster, Matthew McConaughey, Tom Skerritt , James Woods and John Hurt. South Side Amusement Co. 1997.

Grout, Jeff and Perrin, Sarah. <u>Mind Games: Inspirational Lessons from the World's Finest Sports Stars.</u> West Sussex, England. Capstone Publishing Limited, 2006.

Jung, Carl. <u>The Structure and Dynamics of the Psyche</u>. New York. Routledge, 1970.

Pele. <u>My Life and Beautiful Game</u>. New York. Doubleday Books, 1977.

<u>The Silence of the Lambs</u>. Dir. by Jonathan Demme. Prod. by Ron Bozman. Writ.by Thomas Harris. Perf. By Jodie Foster, Anthony Hopkins, Scott Glenn. Orion, 1991.

<u>The Sixth Sense</u>. Dir.by M. Night Shyamala. Prod. by Kathleen Kennedy. Perf. by Bruce Willis, Haley Joel Osment and Toni Collette. Spyglass Entertainment, 1999.

Takatoka. "Noquisi and the Bird" (Reprinted with permission of the Manataka American Indian Council. http://www.manataka.org/page 294.html).

Twain, Mark. <u>The Adventures of Huckleberry Finn</u>. New York. P. F. Collier & Son,1918.

Acknowledgements

My journey is supported by so many. I wish I had the space to thank each and every one of you, but you know who you are and know what you mean to me. To those that have had a direct impact on this book, I sincerely love and thank:

• my sons, Matthew and Joseph, who are exposed to and live a very different life than other young men their age. Their insights and support went beyond mere mother/child bonding into an area of pure understanding and love. You guys are my greatest gifts.

• my parents, who provided the foundation for my gifts to grow.

• Denise Sabol, my editor, to whom much is owed. Denise made the reality of this book possible through her professionalism and kindness.

• Willa Ratner, who designed the cover for this book. You did a great job and I truly appreciate your patience.

• Janice A. Orefice Dehn, who helped me publicize and bring this book to so many.

• Kim C., who is always there to help me out and not afraid to point out all that I don't know! I am enjoying sharing our journeys.

• Susan S., who gave me the big "push" and is always there to listen to my endless stories and rambling. I am glad our souls decided to live another life together.

• my friends in the UAE, Europe, the Middle East and Africa. I feel as though I now have family all over the world!

• all of you who have hosted readings or had private readings. You have touched my life by allowing me a peek into your lives. As you were and are healed, so am I. In a large part, this book is a tribute to you.

• my students, here and abroad, you have been terrific teachers. I learned more from you than I could have from any book.

• my spirit guides. You guys are great! Where would I be without your voices in my ears?

• all of you who picked up this book and allowed me to share my soul with you.

• all those spirits who need to be heard and speak through me. I am humbled in your presence.

Above all, with my eyes up to heaven, my utmost gratitude goes to my God, whose Grace fills my senses and my life. I am so blessed and honored to do your work.

To Contact the Author:

If you wish to contact Anna Raimondi or would like more information about this book or her practice, please email her at talkingtodead@aol.com or go to www. AnnaRaimondi.com. Anna appreciates hearing from you and learning of your enjoyment of this book and how it helped you.